HAUNTED SALEM OREGON

TIM KING

Haunted America

Published by Haunted America
A Division of The History Press
Charleston, SC
www.historypress.com

Front cover: Randy Flook, Salem, Oregon.
Back cover: photo by Tim King; *inset*: courtesy of Shelli Pruett of North Hollywood, California.

First published 2018

Manufactured in the United States

ISBN 9781467138130

Library of Congress Control Number: 2018942428

HAUNTED SALEM OREGON

This book is dedicated to the memory of my late parents,
Charles and Nellie King.

CONTENTS

Preface

Ghosts were real to me as a child. I never doubted the possibility that somehow, some way, certain spirits become earthbound. Overwhelming at times, the subject captured my imagination and never let go.

I like to describe my late parents as politically conservative people who were completely open minded to the idea of ghosts and the supernatural.

Charles and Nellie King were fascinating people. They were married in 1941 and spent every day of their lives together, until the day they passed away together. Each had their own amazing stories. My brothers and I were raised with these tales; they were presented as true, and every single one was captivating and scary. My two older brothers, Ken King and Rick King, have always maintained an interest in the supernatural.

My mom was born in Kansas, and that is where she spent her first twelve years before moving to Los Angeles in 1934. In Kansas, at the age of seven, when her parents divorced, my mom was sent to a Catholic boarding school. The stories from this period are riveting.

She talked about a little girl who was very mysterious, a child who rarely spoke and had no friends. My mom was very shy and easily intimidated, so it is not surprising that my mom failed to reach out to the little girl. One night, my mom discovered something about that little girl. It was a mystery that she would never solve or adequately process.

Late at night, getting up to go to the bathroom, my mom heard a ball bouncing in the school gymnasium. She may have been shy, but my mom was very curious, so she quietly walked downstairs and opened the gym door. She assumed, quite logically, that one or more of the kids were breaking the rules and having fun with a ball. But what she observed after opening the door defies all explanation.

The little mystery girl was sitting in the middle of the gym floor with her legs folded, looking as if she was in a trance, my mom recalled. The little girl was repeating the words, "Bounce ball bounce" and a large ball was bouncing consistently about five feet in front of the child. As if that wasn't enough to completely overwhelm my poor mom, the girl looked her straight in the eyes, and my mom said she just melted and ran back to her bed.

Another night, in the same place, my mom got up very late to use the restroom when everyone was asleep. She was confronted by the ghost of a woman wearing all white. She said she screamed and ran back to the dormitory as fast as she could. It was later determined that the lady my mom saw was probably one of the nuns in a white nightgown, but she never got over it. Those moments were burned into my mom's memory.

While my dad was growing up, he had the unique fortune of spending a great deal of time on my family ranch in the Chino Valley of California. As a child, I had the same opportunity, though to a much lesser extent.

My dad, who was born in 1917, was raised during the final years of the property being an active cattle ranch. I was raised with heaping amounts of family history and lore. Even today, my family ranch in Chino is still an active component of California history; it is a preserved state museum called the Yorba-Slaughter Adobe.

One night, around 1931 or so, my dad and his good friend Tom Core were taking a midnight walk on the road that led to the adobe. Walking past the foundation of an earlier ancestor's homesite, they saw a light in the sky illuminating a field.

When my dad and his friend got closer, they saw that there was an undefinable object in the sky creating a circle of light about forty, possibly fifty feet in diameter. He said that if you stepped into the light, everything was like daylight. They heard no sound coming from whatever was generating the light, but they estimated the object to be about fifty feet in the air.

There was never an explanation for what it was that they saw that night. An earlier look at family history reveals that in the 1870s, a cigar-shaped object that reportedly had people inside, waving to those they passed, flew through the Chino Valley and was witnessed by hundreds of people. While balloons certainly were flying for quite some time by the 1870s, longer airships, zeppelins and dirigibles would not debut for many years.

My dad talked about an even stranger night that involved both he and his friend Tom. They were both around fourteen, taking another one of their midnight walks, when they looked over to the milk house and saw one of the ranch hands inside. They didn't think too much about it.

The next morning, at breakfast, my father and his friend described seeing the ranch hand, whose name was Tom, in the milk house. My dad's uncle Hode angrily demanded to know what they were talking about. "You know damned well milk houses don't have windows." As it turned out, my dad and his friend could not possibly have seen a window or light, because the milk house was simply a concrete building, no way to see out or in. Yet they did. What forces or powers were at work that night?

Another story that my mom always shared was about an extremely strange event one night in Northern California. She believed always that a Bigfoot or Sasquatch approached them when they were sleeping in their camper in an extremely remote location known for sightings of the creature.

My mom and my oldest brother were awakened by a foul smell. They both recall that there had been cows near them when they went to sleep, and the cowbells were audible and even a relaxing and comforting sound. Then, just as the smell became prominent, the cows began to run away, their bells falling silent very quickly. The smell seeping into their camper from outside became worse.

My mom said she tried to wake my dad and have him get one of his rifles, but he was fast asleep, and he jokingly told her to go back to sleep. Then, to my mom's horror, whatever it was outside brushed up against the camper. My mom thought she could hear its breath. The next morning, my mom was unhappy with my dad. They never told me whether or not they looked for footprints. Those are the kind of stories I was raised with.

Another night, long before my time, my parents were camping in the desert. To break the boredom, they would do this strange thing with a card table. Everyone placed their hands on top of it and said, "Rise, table, rise." One night, both of my parents explained, the table simply lifted into the air and then floated away from them, moving several feet into the desert. None of their hands were on or even near the table.

I believe that the stories my parents shared absolutely ignited a flame inside my heart and have largely been responsible for my continued interest in things that are supernatural and impossible to explain. These stories set the stage for a lifetime of interest and research into the paranormal world.

In my career, I have written and produced a number of articles and reports about paranormal research and ghost stories. The first time I merged my supernatural interest with broadcasting was when I served as news director for KLYC, 1260 AM in McMinnville, Oregon. As the news director, I was the first to arrive each morning and begin the station's broadcast day at 6:00 a.m. Adjacent to the DJ booth was an area we called the rack room, where the broadcast equipment and controls were located. My first act of the day was to "warm up the plates," which sat for roughly fifteen minutes, prior to the moment I activated the transmitter.

Each morning when I was in the rack room, I would see a person or an object moving in my periphery, in my right eye, but whenever I would look up to see it, nothing was there. I admit that I didn't enjoy opening that station each morning, though the vibe throughout the day was very normal and pleasant. This station allowed me to explore the paranormal subject in detail, and I learned a great deal from a clairvoyant I worked with. She taught me a number of things about the relationship between news media and paranormal studies.

One of the first things reporters learn about the supernatural is that it is of strong interest to mainstream media during exactly two weeks of the year, those of course being the final two weeks in October.

Knight Hall Ghost

I fell into the game of paying attention to the supernatural during those weeks initially while working for KLYC, and it happened to be October 1991, so I chose to follow a story from the *Oregonian* newspaper about a haunted building at Pacific University in Forest Grove, Oregon, called Knight Hall.

I tracked down an extremely talented Portland psychic named Erin Laselle, who had been quoted by the *Oregonian* about the ghost of a girl who had been talked about for decades at Knight Hall, affectionately known as Vera.[1]

I asked her to come to the radio station to do an hour-long live talk show about the supernatural. After the show, I gave her a tour of the radio station. She said that because our tower was right outside the station's door, she could not decipher the source of the haunting, but she said there was definitely something there. We got into my station's bright-orange KLYC van and drove to Pacific University to investigate the Knight Hall ghost.

I had called the university ahead of time, and Erin and I were welcomed. We went to Knight Hall. We became situated on one of the stairway landings.

We sat down, and Erin almost immediately went into a trance-like state. She explained what she was seeing and hearing, and I took notes.

Erin talked about a young woman who had lived in the house; she believed her to be the daughter of the first president of the university, which takes us back to the mid- to late 1800s. She said the young woman had been sexually abused by her father and that she took her own life in the house after discovering that she had conceived his child.

Erin said the father died in front of the house about a year after that, adding that he had been trampled to death in a horse-and-buggy accident. She said the girl roamed the house freely, adding that she definitely didn't like Erin looking at her. Erin had the distinct impression that the girl did not like other females, and more than fifty years of student and staff observations absolutely concurred; the ghost was friendly toward males, not so friendly toward females.

Erin added repeatedly that they were buried "right over there." Unfortunately, she continued to point at a large, multistory school building.

After being on the landing for some time, a student approached us and asked if we would visit with one of the music professors, a woman we will simply call Ruth, which we gladly agreed to do. The professor was a very elegant middle-aged woman who badly wanted to get something off of her chest. She told us that she was going to share an experience that she had never told anyone about.

About a year earlier, she had been very close to a newly arrived professor of music who was just out of school. The younger professor was struck by a car one afternoon in McMinnville and died a few hours later from her injuries. Ruth had to open Knight Hall the next morning, and she was devastated.

A couple of students arrived early that morning so Ruth would not be alone. As they entered Knight Hall, the favorite music of the recently deceased professor was neatly arranged on tables immediately inside the building. Ruth said she was the only person who could possibly have known that the music comprised all of the woman's favorites. She was immediately convinced that it was a message from her fallen friend.

The next thing Ruth noticed was a distinct draft coming from upstairs. A little dazed and shaken, Ruth proceeded upstairs and found a window on the third floor open. It was the type of window that opens outward and is held in place by a pair of chains, one on each side.

As Ruth reached up to close it, the most frightening, impossible thing happened. Against all possible laws of physics, the window slammed shut and then fell open again. "I thought I was going to have a heart attack right on the spot," she told us. Needless to say, the window could never have slammed shut; the weight of the window holds it open.

We thanked the professor for sharing her story and headed for the university's museum, hoping to make contact with the school archivist. The archivist had plenty of information. He said the most startling thing as he pointed toward the building that Erin kept referencing—the early residents and school founders were buried in a cemetery that, school officials feared, was not relocated when the building was constructed.

Stories like this make paranormal investigation highly addictive. In later years, while working as a photojournalist/reporter for KATU Channel 2, the ABC affiliate for Portland, Oregon, I produced a number of reports about haunted locations in Oregon.

BRINGING GHOSTS HOME

One KATU report was about what happens to paranormal investigators after they immerse themselves in haunted environments and then go home. Not surprisingly, they have a tendency to bring home spiritual hitchhikers.

A group out of Wilsonville, Oregon, watched moving orbs occupy their hallway for more than forty-five minutes. Orbs are silvery gray round objects that show up in photos taken in haunted environments. The quick-thinking paranormal team recorded it all on videotape.

I then took the footage, had it analyzed and created a three-minute report for our newscast. That story sat on the front page of KATU.com for six months, with people voting whether or not they believed the report was a true indicator of ghosts.

GHOSTS OF AN AFGHAN CASTLE

On other occasions I reported fascinating, offbeat stories, including a report on the haunted Khayr Kot Castle in Afghanistan, where I stayed briefly in 2006.

This amazing castle had been built by the British during their second war in Afghanistan in the late 1800s. The British eventually left and allowed the castle to fall into ruin. It took another bloody conflict for the castle to regain its importance.

Khayr Kot was restored by Soviet forces after they invaded Afghanistan in 1979 at the start of another bitter, protracted war in the nation. The Russians used it as a place to imprison, torture, rape and murder their victims.[2]

People who live nearby said a loved one would go missing and then their screams would be heard coming from the castle. None were ever seen again.

A U.S. Navy sailor took me on a tour of the castle. He showed me the graffiti scrawled inside the towers. It dated back to the Brits in the nineteenth century and included signatures of Soviet soldiers, plenty of Arabic writing and, of course, the modern stuff from the Americans. The guy told me the place was extremely haunted and the soldiers there saw apparitions frequently.

While I was only there for a night and didn't witness anything personally, the place gave off a feeling that was unmistakably haunting.

So What Is a Ghost?

Experts explain that there are several different types of ghosts. Among the different categories are intelligent ghosts, residual spirits, poltergeists, demonic ghosts and shadow people.

It is important to remember that just because something goes bump in the night it is not necessarily a ghost. Most things that seem abnormal, I firmly believe, do in fact have a simple, scientific answer.

The most interesting type of ghost—which always draws strong interest—is what we call an intelligent ghost. This is the spirit of a person who died unexpectedly and was unable to accept their death or move on into the realm of death. Instead, they remain left behind as an earthbound spirit. These spirits often seek to make contact with living people. In some cases, they died with a secret that they want to reveal.

It is important to remember that ghosts do not have rules or parameters. They can travel and roam at will, though most tend to stay in one place (though ghosts have been known to follow people to their home or another location). It seems entirely possible that ghosts can become fixated on particular people.

Another type of entity that people frequently experience is a residual ghost. This is entirely different from an intelligent ghost and, in all likelihood, is not a ghost at all. These entities seem more than anything else to repeat the movements that the person they appear as conducted on a regular basis in their lifetimes.

Salem is known for several residual ghosts, including the transparent image of a man who approaches the front of the historic Elsinore Theater and disappears as he reaches the stage. This sight has been witnessed by many people over the years. The man reportedly walks where people are seated rather than using an aisle, and he seems to begin at the knees, as if his feet are on another plain. Perhaps the Elsinore's floors were raised over the years? As the man reaches the stage, he simply vanishes. This vision has been reported for many years.

Another residual ghost in Salem is connected to a store owner who ran one of the city's busiest general stores in the 1870s. It is said that the elderly owner always tapped on the windows with his cane as he approached the store. This was his signal of arrival to ensure that employees appeared busy and working as he entered the building. To this day, people who rent the old store will almost always end up approaching the building's owners asking why, at 9:00 a.m., like clockwork, the knocking sounds ring out.

By all accounts, residual ghosts are simply repeating actions from their mortal lives. In every case that I have studied, they never attempt to make contact with people or recognize any living human beings.

Demonic hauntings are the ones that most investigators tend to avoid. These are actually possessed ghosts; they tend to exist in environments where several ghosts exist together. Demonic spirits will frighten and intimidate other ghosts, and they have a propensity to prevent other entities from leaving or moving on.

In my early years following paranormal investigators and documenting investigations, I learned about the "Casper syndrome." We all remember Casper the Friendly Ghost as a cartoon. It was funny and entertaining, and poor Casper was always singled out and picked on by the mean ghosts. I have covered different stories about haunted buildings that have multiple spirits.

The Casper syndrome reflects the simple fact that ghosts have a hierarchy just like living people. I like to think they are not demonic simply because they are mean. I reason that ghosts carry on some of the characteristics of the human beings they once were.

Interestingly, demonic spirits also seem to double as poltergeists, with the ability to move and manipulate objects in our mortal world.

The poltergeist, or "noisy ghost," is, in my opinion, an entity that has been around long enough to learn to manipulate objects in our physical world.

They frequently relocate objects that people are looking for. Poltergeists turn lights off and on and like to hide keys and other items that a person will predictably need and seek out.

Less is known about shadow people. Some experts speculate that they are simply unable to show anything about themselves except for the shadowy outline. Some shadow people wear hats or what appears to be the outline of a hat. These entities are often seen in a person's peripheral vision, and they move or disappear when a person turns their head to look at them.

USUALLY EXPLAINABLE

I tell people who attend my ghost tours about a night that I was followed by unusual lights while driving a rental car back to Paris, France.

Having been in the field for days, conducting World War I battlefield research, I admit I was already a bit spooked when this strange event happened. I mean, *all* of Europe seems so old and different when compared to the United States. But these lights, one on either side of my car, moved around and just seemed fixated on the vehicle. I could speed up or slow down, but nothing shook these lights that were seemingly riveted on my every move.

Fairly convinced that I was experiencing something highly unusual if not supernatural, I took an exit and went into a French boutique, or convenience store. The clerk didn't speak English, and I know only a handful of words and phrases in French, but he followed along with what I was asking and replied "discotheque" while pointing in the direction I was traveling.

I thanked him and continued down the freeway, when I observed on the left side, in a massive field, a large-scale rave party with huge spotlights pointing into the low, cloud-laden sky. I immediately knew that the lights following my car were nothing but reflections from the rave's spotlights. As mysterious as they were, like most things, there was a logical explanation.

It is when you encounter things that cannot in any scientific way be possible that you start to see the actual paranormal side of our world.

I frequently explain to people that when an eighty-five-year-old grandfather is passing, they do so knowing they have completed their assignment on earth. These folks don't usually cling to the earth in a panic. They simply allow the process to happen.

Now, don't get me wrong, plenty of elderly people seem to become ghosts, too, but it seems there are often extenuating circumstances in those cases.

A friend of mine on the Oregon coast years ago lived with the ghost of the cranky old man who had owned the house before she bought it. She could sense a possessive nature to his spirit and found his presence to be mean and unkind, as well as disrespectful. The man's ghost would actually crawl into bed with her at night, and the basement of the house was completely uncomfortable.

She learned a bit about the old codger. This was not your typically happy senior citizen; he was a man who had much difficulty in his life. He had lost his wife and been forgotten by his children. His lingering existence could be tied to the misery he experienced in his lifetime.

From everything we know, those who die and move on can return to pay a visit. This does not mean the person is earthbound or relegated to this planet.

If your lost loved one begins making regular appearances, particularly at some predictable intervals in time, they may be a ghost.

Ghosts seem to originate from many sources. Not only people of all ages, but animals also seem to have the same experience.

From the beginning of audio recording, people have been documenting the voices of ghosts, typically referred to as electronic voice phenomena or EVPs. Animal EVPs are not uncommon. Some are more than startling and seem extremely responsive to questions asked of them by paranormal investigators.

1
The Chinese Are Still Underground

A labyrinth of tunnels snakes its way under Salem's old downtown section. Light still filters in through the sidewalk skylights, which are often tainted purple from age.

These dark underground passageways were used by the public to navigate between buildings in the late nineteenth century and a good part of the twentieth century. There was a main tunnel system and numerous catacombs, many of which still exist.

The tunnel system began at Salem's busy riverfront and led to any number of popular locations. Underground tunnels were dug by the Chinese, who were frequently relegated to an underground existence.

An interesting fact about the Chinese, according to SalemHistory.net, is that many who immigrated to the United States feared finding themselves in a barbaric place, so they brought many comforts from home, including dishes, cutlery, clothes and food. Rice could be purchased locally, but many Chinese still came prepared. Chinese also brought opium, which had been brought out of India by the British and introduced to the Chinese.

Chinese made good money compared to what they could earn in China. In fact, an average worker in the United States in the 1870s earned roughly five times what he or she would have earned at home. Still, much resentment existed toward this population, because in almost any event, Chinese were willing to work for less than white Americans.

Chinese began moving into the Salem area in the 1870s. There were 367 Chinese people living in Marion County, Oregon, in 1890.[3] That number

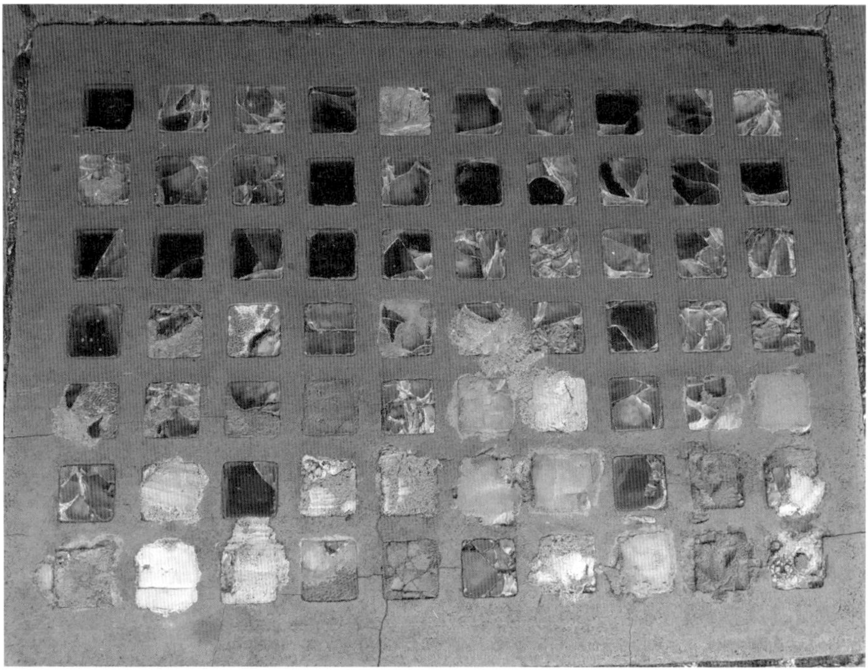

The skylights in the sidewalk at the Bike Peddler show wear and age but are no less intriguing. *Photo by Austin King.*

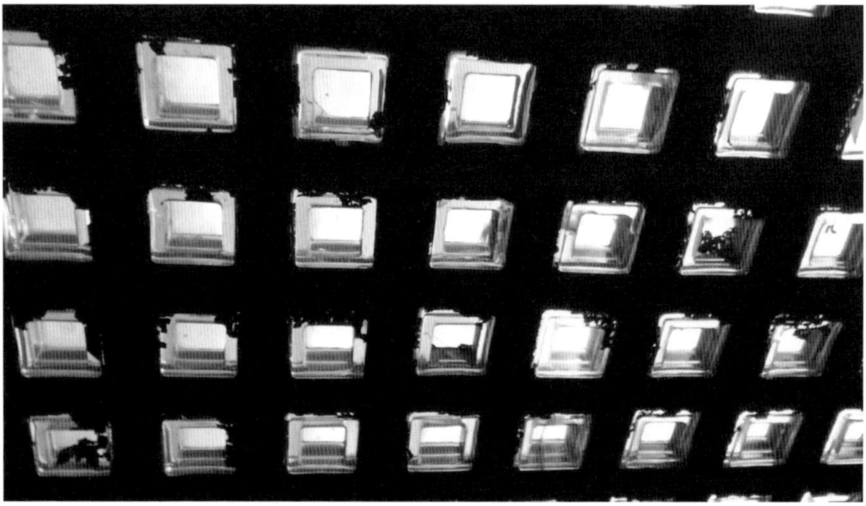

Beneath one of Salem's sidewalk skylights. *Photo by Tim King.*

fell to 235 in 1900. By 1910, the Chinese had regained numbers here, and 288 people were counted. In 1920, according to figures from the U.S. Bureau of Labor, there were 72 Chinese residents in the county, earning an average of $800 a year.

Chinese were not citizens, and they could not vote or own land or mineral rights. They faced serious discrimination, though Salem was a better place for Chinese than was Portland, where hostilities against them were intense and attacks on the streets were not uncommon.

That isn't to suggest that Chinese didn't have problems in Salem. Resentment and opposition toward this race went public in 1873, when the editor of the *Salem Weekly Mercury* voiced his concern over Republicans constituting the board of county commissioners. He charged, "It employs Chinese to work the county roads. White men are plenty and need the work."

The media always has the potential to create societal discomfort. Newspapers in the old days were frequently racist and created as platforms to build political careers. The *Oregonian* in Portland had a racist editor, Harvey W. Scott. He said Chinese were only capable of menial labor. He resented the fact that the majority of Chinese did not assimilate into U.S. culture.

Chinese in Salem worked in a variety of capacities, including railroad construction, land clearing, road construction and agriculture. In many cases, they worked as servants and tradesmen.

The Underground

Many stories emanate from the underground, and rumors of lifeless forms moving in the dark shadows have never ceased.

Today, quite sadly, much of Salem's underground has been filled in. Long passageways that had access to spacious rooms only accessible through the underground tunnels are now blocked off and filled in. Before they were filled in, historians mapped out the most interesting tunnels along State Street, Court Street and Liberty Street in downtown Salem. All efforts to preserve the tunnels failed.

One story explains how bizarre and obscure Salem's underground is.

A few years ago, a local retired professor found the remains of an opium den in a tunnel on State Street, just prior to the restoration of the McGilchrist Building, which was erected in 1916. During this historic discovery, he

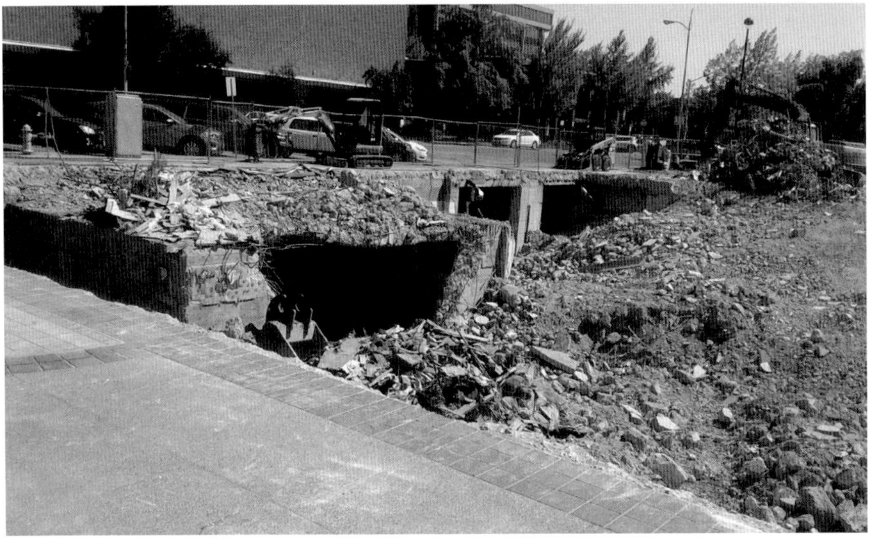

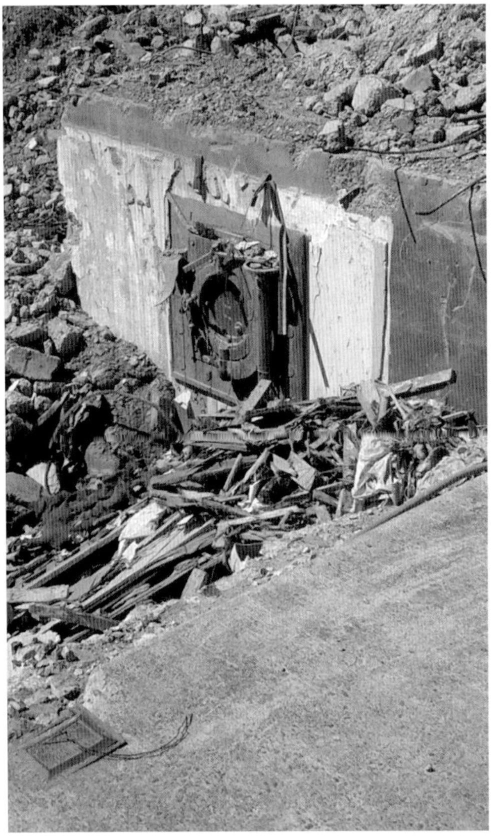

Above: A recently demolished building in downtown Salem reveals its underground passageways. *Photo by Brittany Anne Dow.*

Left: A building recently demolished in downtown Salem reveals its historic past, including what appears to be a safe. *Photo by Brittany Anne Dow.*

actually recovered an opium pipe, estimated to be from 1880. The same historians attained permission to open a door in the back of McGilchrist that had not been opened in decades. Opening the door, they found a long, dark flight of stairs. At the bottom of the stairs, on the underground level, was a long-forgotten discotheque, complete with a sparkling silver ball over a sunken dance floor and dusty, high-backed red booths.

That is an inside look at the bizarre, hidden history that resides under Salem's streets, sidewalks and buildings—an opium pipe from 1880 on one side of the underground wall, and a 1980 disco long vanished from memory on the other. Other discoveries beneath Salem included storefronts, archways, an underground grocery store, rooms with murals painted on the walls and the business of a furrier, where an 1870 bear trap was found.

A recent report on KPTV FOX 12 in Portland showed the discovery of yet another opium den under a pair of old Salem buildings.[4] The ventilators in the ceiling where more than a hundred years ago people exhaled opium smoke are still in place. Opium is the only nefarious activity that was absolutely relegated to the underground. It was a popular pastime in Salem

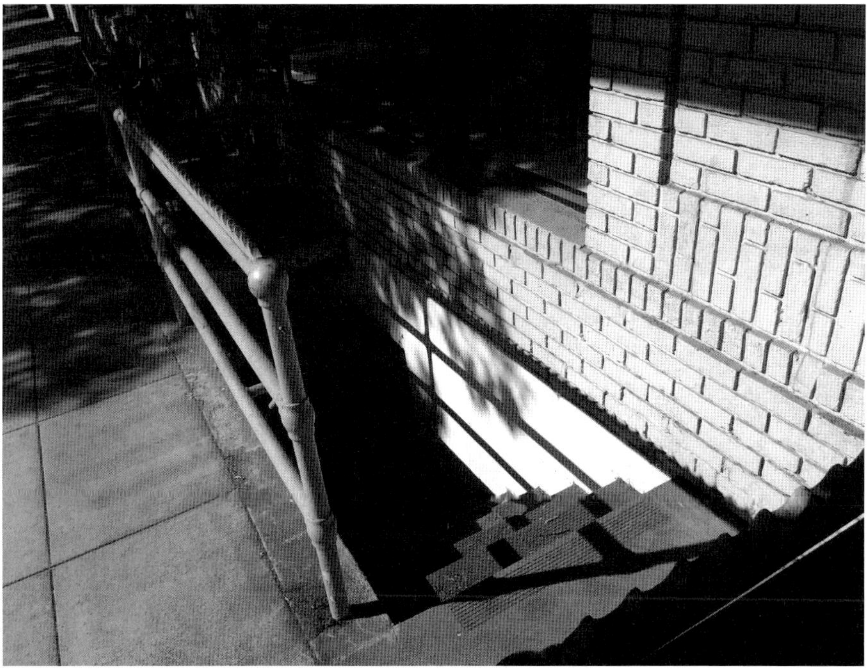

Stairs leading to the underground comfort station beneath the sidewalks of the Oregon Building. *Photo by Brittany Anne Dow.*

for many years. That's right, Salem, like so many cities of the Old West, had a serious drug problem that plagued many of its residents.

One underground section in Salem contains the remains of an expansive set of restrooms, or, as they were known at the time, "comfort stations." In 1917, the facilities were created under the Oregon Building at the intersection of High and State Streets. The facility is located catty-corner from the Marion County Courthouse. Massive skylights in the sidewalk allowed daylight to illuminate the underground restrooms. Proper facilities in downtown Salem are hard to come by. The awareness of the need to maintain public restrooms was not lost on Salem's early leaders. Today, a handful of business and community leaders maintain art-decorated "porta potties," a far cry from Salem's publicly funded 1917 comfort station. A set of stairs leading down to the old facility is still in place today, though it has not been used in many years.

A Harrowing Encounter

A story was related to me at the close of one of my weekend ghost tours. In the early 1970s, the tunnel systems were used by young people who wanted a safe and out-of-the-way place to party and cut loose. It had to have been thrilling to go into a subterranean chamber that had been so long abandoned. However, this group of four high school revelers ended up with something they did not expect: uninvited company.

After entering the underground tunnels through one of the access points, the group of teens—three boys and one girl—found an extremely interesting area dimly lit by their flashlights. It was a former underground storefront. I have independently verified that these areas exist/existed prominently throughout the former underground commerce area.

It was not revealed to me specifically, but I got the impression during my conversation with the man after my tour that the group may have taken LSD, or "acid"—never ever a good idea when dealing with ancillary energy such as a ghost. After a couple of hours, the four were extremely surprised to see another person in the underground with them. The man described a girl wearing unusual clothing.

This was the early 1970s, but the girl looked like she was dressed in garb from the 1920s or earlier. He said they all fell silent when she appeared. For several minutes, the girl who, appeared to be roughly the same age as these high school students, simply looked at the group from the shadows. She appeared lost, and her eyes seemed to be vacant.

All four of the teenagers saw her. No one knew how to respond. When spoken to, she didn't acknowledge or return their greeting. She did appear near one of the sidewalk skylights, which, I was told, added a purplish tint to her whitish face.

"The strangest thing about it," the man told me, "is that the girl eventually disappeared into the shadows." He said there was no possible way she could have seen enough to navigate the tunnels without a flashlight or torch.

That is one of many creepy stories about the underground tunnels downtown. Even the Salem police have questions about remaining tunnel sections. It is likely that there are stretches of the tunnel system that still exist but are undocumented and completely mysterious.

Salem's waterfront was sizable, covering an area that began near downtown and continued for miles along Front Street. Insiders say there were tunnels constructed along the entire way.

Underground Graveyard?

The stories of Salem's underground are varied, yet they always convey the creepiness and loneliness of the dark passages that have been quiet for so long.

People often ask me during my ghost tours, "Why doesn't Salem offer underground tours like Portland, Seattle, Pendleton and Sacramento?" I generally explain that Salem is yet to have a city council with that type of vision. I suspect the city officials fear liability, but there is another, rather intriguing theory that could well explain why the city is so reluctant to acknowledge or preserve the tunnels.

The U.S. Census Bureau documented more than three hundred Chinese residents in Salem in the 1870s. It is fair to assume that it missed people. So, where are the graves of these Chinese that should number in the hundreds?

Some speculate that Salem's underground doubled as a burial spot for Chinese who passed during the difficult years, when a law called the Chinese Exclusion Act was passed after the completion of the transcontinental railroad system.

We may never know, but a close review of Salem's cemeteries hold only a scant number of Chinese graves. Are the Chinese still underground?

SIDEWALK SKYLIGHTS: WINDOWS TO THE PAST

Skylights in the sidewalks are found all over downtown Salem, and you will find similar skylights in sidewalks from Astoria and Portland, all the way to Coos Bay. The skylights of downtown Salem are a remarkable reminder of past years, when life flourished underground.

The purple color of the skylight glass is a direct indicator of its age. I remember how excited my mom would get when we explored old ghost towns and mines and she would discover purple glass. It means that we were dealing with something from many years ago.

In the mid-1800s, glass makers began adding manganese dioxide, which was nicknamed "glassmaker's soap." This caused glass to lose its natural green tint and become colorless.

An 1899 publication by Benjamin Biser, "Elements of Glass and Glass Making," explains why manganese dioxide was used. "The especial use of manganese in glass is to mask or neutralize the greenish color imparted to the glass by the protoxide of iron.[5] Manganese imparts to glass a pink or red

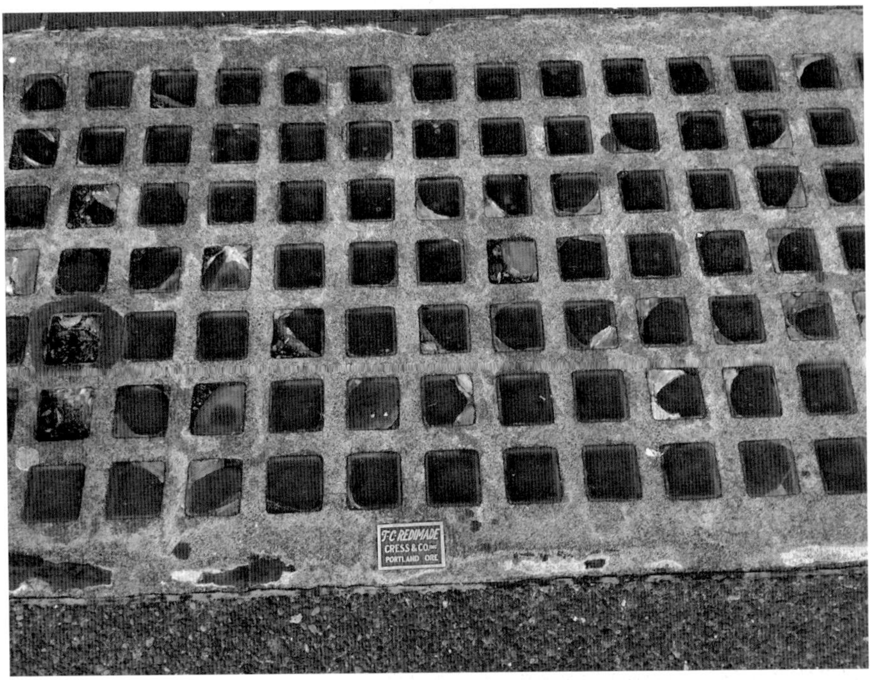

Many people walk by these skylight panels their whole lives and never realize they are walking over ancient underground passageways. *Photo by Brittany Anne Dow.*

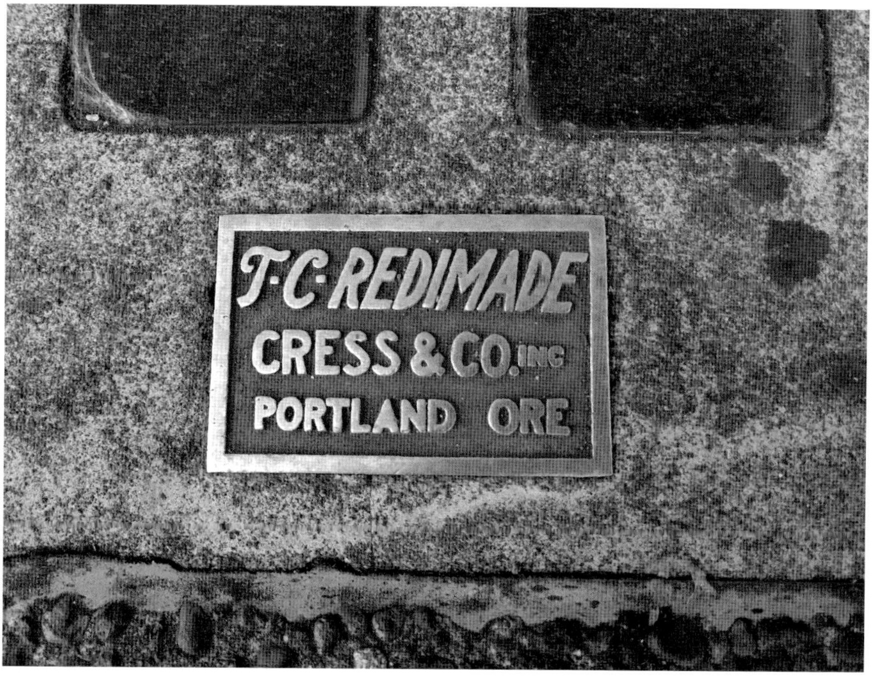

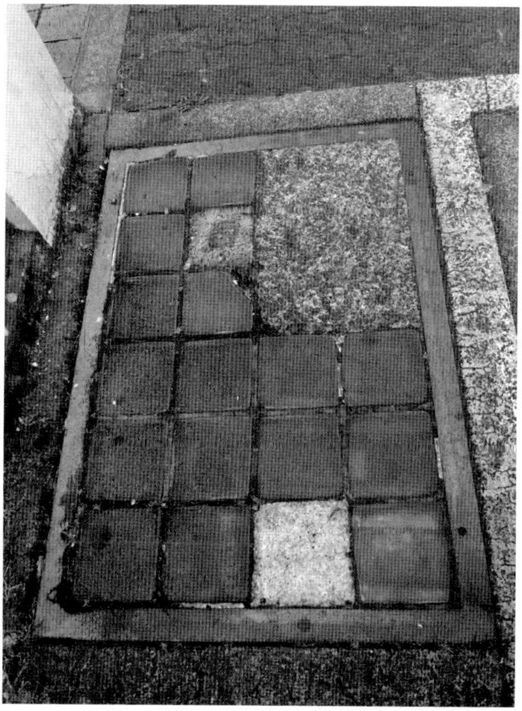

Above: Though its products have changed, a sidewalk skylight manufacturer in Portland is still in business. *Photo by Tim King.*

Left: Underground skylights like these are found in Salem's alleys. They are different than the sidewalk skylights. They are clear, unlike the purple glass panels in the sidewalk skylights. *Photo by Brittany Anne Dow.*

tint, which being complementary to green, neutralizes the color and permits the glass to transmit white light."

The manganese process ended after the close of World War I, but all over the West Coast, sidewalks still hold these often beautiful glass skylights. Salem skylights were manufactured by Cress & Company, a historic Portland company that has been in business for more than 120 years.

Scott Cress, the current president and third-generation owner of W.H. Cress, says the company was founded 122 years ago, and while he never dealt specifically with the skylights, he is very familiar with them. "I had a phone call about ten years ago from a guy who said he had one of these things but it was in awful shape. I told him our company no longer had any of those and wished him luck, it was very interesting."

Scott Cress emphasized that there used to be a large number of glass covers, or skylights, throughout Portland. I explained to Scott that a lady attending my ghost tour from Coos Bay said the exact skylights were in place there. I also noted that the skylights in Astoria are also like dead ringers.

Another unique type of skylight is found in Salem's alleys. These are larger glass panels that have not turned purple over the years. They show us that the underground tunnels continued down the alleyways of the city as well.

MORE SALEM TUNNELS

I would not be surprised if Salem qualified as a record holder for the largest number of underground tunnels in a U.S. city.

The network of tunnels downtown is just the beginning. As the state capital, Salem hosts a large number of state buildings in what is known as the "Capital mall." The buildings continue in different directions for several blocks. All of the state buildings are connected through underground tunnels. The tunnels are primarily for evacuation purposes. They are maintained, and designated people in each of the buildings are key carriers who are charged with unlocking the passageways in the event of an evacuation.

The Oregon State Penitentiary is connected via dark, mysterious tunnels to the Oregon State Hospital. The state hospital tunnels are notorious and long known for their ghostly presence. They roam under Salem streets and, I am told, directly through some neighborhoods in northeast Salem.

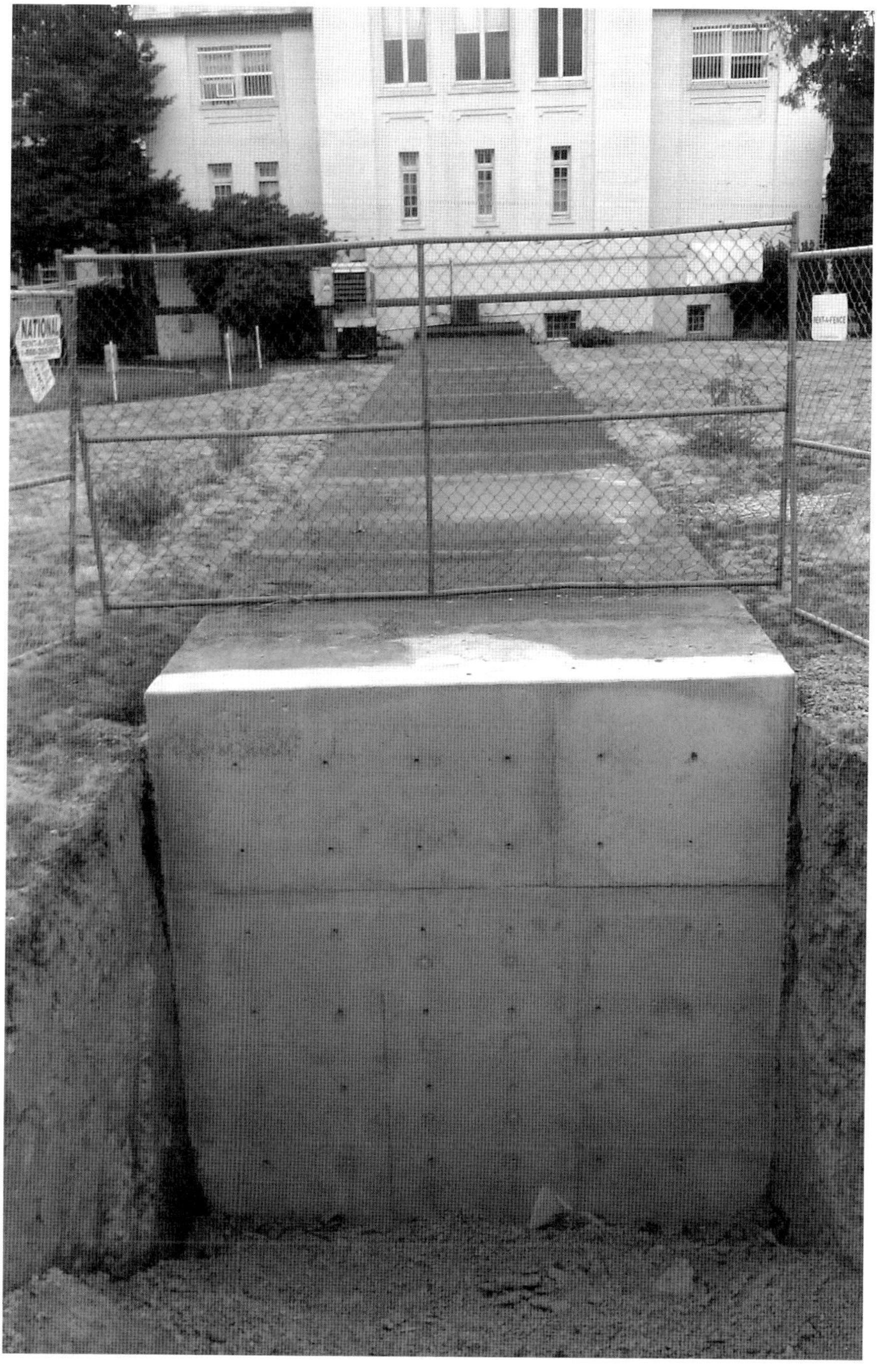

A filled-in tunnel section at Oregon State Hospital. *Photo by Brittany Anne Dow.*

The Fairview property has miles of tunnels that are still intact and largely available to see on YouTube. People have recorded quality EVPs in these tunnel systems. It is hard to imagine the years when people were forced to use these tunnels to travel between the various buildings.

Corban University, formerly Western Baptist in Salem, exists at the old Oregon Tuberculosis Hospital, one of the first taxpayer-funded tuberculosis hospitals in the nation. Of course, why did people go to a tuberculosis hospital? For only one reason: to die. Once a visitor to the campus knows the story, the place takes on another feeling.

Years ago, when I was with KATU, I interviewed the incoming president of the university, who showed me a tunnel opening that was very close to the old buildings on the campus. As I recall, there was an actual doorway and two doors that opened from the center; the tunnel struck me as something that must have been used regularly at one point in the school/facility's history. The new university president also was fascinated by the knowledge.

I returned once to try to locate that tunnel opening a few years later, but security guards made our search impossible Nonetheless, within the Salem landscape, even Corban University and the old tuberculosis hospital were the scene of a maze of tunnels.

2

Political Specters of the Statehouse

The Oregon state capitol is reputed to be haunted by a series of entities that roam the hallways at night.

Today's statehouse occupies the space where not one but two previous capitol buildings existed. Both of the previous structures were lost in fires. In fact, that is the story of many Salem buildings. The first capitol building went up in flames in 1855, before the governor, George Law Curry, had officially taken a seat at his desk.

Many believe that the capitol building attracts ghosts because they return to places they once knew and frequented, and the capitol is a busy place on any weekday, particularly when the legislature is in session. But if you find yourself alone in the middle of the night in the capitol building, as I did on several occasions while working for Portland ABC station KATU, the odds of experiencing something inexplicable go way up.

It was a weeknight, about two o'clock in the morning, back in 2003, when I was called out to cover a fatal crash on the interstate. These are always tragic experiences, and that night I was the only media representative present. We try to get those key shots that tell the story, and sometimes our camera records things that we would never want the viewing audience to see.

This was one of those nights.

As a human being, I never stopped being fully impacted by fatal incidents like this, regardless of how many different deaths I had covered. I always felt the loss and was humbled to be present in the wake of any person's passing.

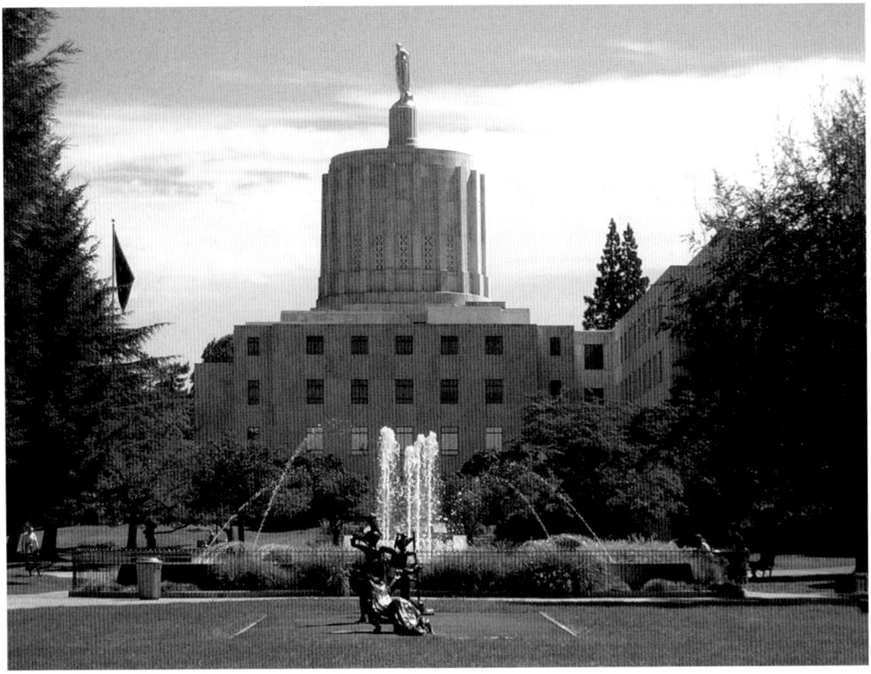

The Oregon State Capitol grounds in Salem. *Photo by Tim King.*

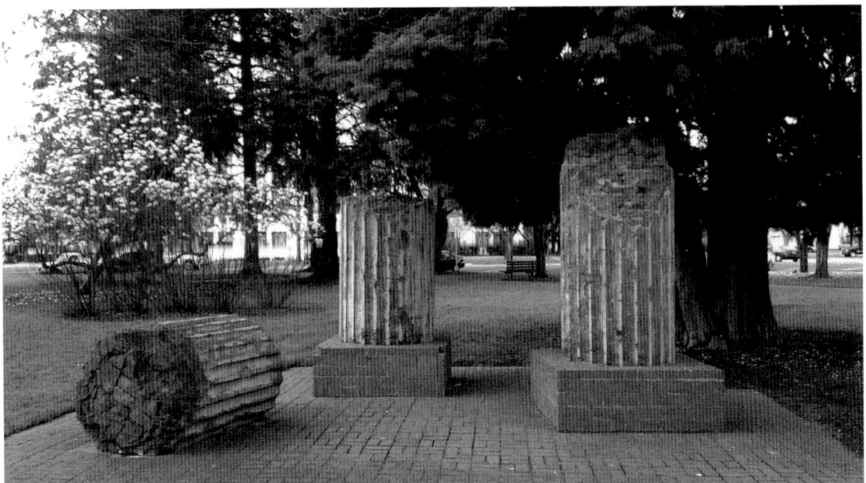

Columns that once stood in front of the Oregon State Capitol building, which burned in 1935. *Photo by Tim King.*

After leaving the scene of the crash, I drove to the capitol and let myself in the east-side door with my capitol building ID card. I was very new and didn't know my way around the capitol very well yet. I entered the elevator and while riding down to the media bureau in the capitol's basement was touched by a human hand on my shoulder!

This is the kind of feeling you can readily identify. It was the firm press of a human hand when there was not another person anywhere near me. I wasn't alarmed, but it was an unnerving experience. I felt fingers. I was already shaken from the fatal crash I had just covered. It really makes my mind wander when I look back at that night.

This personal experience certainly helps explain some stories, like the one about the cleaning lady who felt a man place his hand on her shoulder, only to turn around and see a former Oregon senator standing in front of her. The senator had perished in a car crash a couple of years before. The maid picked him out of a photo lineup after being so frightened by the vision that she was ready to quit her job on the spot.

I think a hand being placed on a shoulder is a gentle type of contact, if you are going to have one. It certainly would not be pleasant if the hand was placed around my neck. It did not seem threatening, but it did strike me as an act from a lonely soul.

Footsteps in the Night

The Oregon capitol is a place where people walk by you with sharp, distinct steps—when there is no one to be seen. This is one of the more frequently reported experiences in the building. The elevator where I felt a hand on my shoulder is a place where many have had odd experiences that defy explanation.

Another story related by an employee at the capitol involves the figure of a man who is standing in the gallery. The man, or what appeared to be a man, had his hands on the railing and was staring down at the employee.

The employee, who made an official report about what he witnessed, added that the man, or figure, had no clear features on his face. This is noted in many similar photos, where the ghost may be perfectly definable, even unmistakably definable, and yet their faces seem to be a void.

Another story that always held my attention involved a security guard working alone at night in the capitol building. He was standing near the center kiosk when he distinctly heard a man walking toward him. Assuming that there was a person in the building—even though no human being except him was present—the guard followed the sound of the steps. He heard them moving toward a stairway. They were very distinctive.

The security guard continued following the sound all the way to the House chambers, which are always kept locked at night. He said they moved quickly. As the chamber doors came into view, the security guard distinctly heard and saw the doors slam closed. The doors, he said, were always kept locked.

The capitol is connected to underground tunnels, one leading from the parking garage on Chemeketa Street Northeast to the capitol building. One night, an Oregon state police trooper pulled into a parking space and then noticed a swirling ball of energy that was fluorescent green.

The trooper snapped a photo of the object, known as an *ectoplasm*—believed to be a viscous substance of supernatural origin that represents a spirit. The photo surprisingly didn't record the ectoplasm itself, but it did reveal three bright-green figures that appear as people with their heads bowed.

Numerous state employees who work in the capitol have shared stories about odd things taking place in the building. While taking one of my ghost tours, a local resident who worked in the capitol one summer related how she was setting up displays after the building was closed. Items were falling from her table—"being knocked from my table" in her words.

She said it started basically from the moment she began her work there. Her colleagues had similar experiences. They all found the work environment a chilling one.

3
GHOSTS OF THE HANGING GROUND

In the 1800s and early 1900s, people in the United States would pack their children, make a picnic lunch and travel, often long distances, to witness a hanging.

Of course, hangings were never a nice thing to see. Plenty of children surely had a jolting moment when a man would hit the end of the rope, his neck often snapping—but not always. Sometimes, the hanged man would suffer, his feet writhing in a grotesque dance of sorts while his life energy dissipated.

Salem's hanging ground, where men lost their lives in a grim public spectacle, existed within Pringle Park, on the south bank of Mill Creek, a few hundred feet north of Pringle Creek. This is close to both Willamette University and the enclosed parking structure for the SAIF Building.

The first time I walked onto the grounds of Pringle Park, it was Halloween night the first year I moved to Salem. I took my boys to the park to see a Halloween event, with people dressed as part of a living history exhibit. It was chilling and breathtaking. I recall one of my boys not being convinced that these were all living people dressed up in celebration of Halloween.

Perhaps it is the history of the hangings or the rich native lore surrounding this treasured part of Salem, but you can feel spiritual energy in Pringle Park, particularly at night. "If there were any site in Salem that should be haunted, it's the location on lower Church Street that served as the town's hanging ground in the early years."[6]

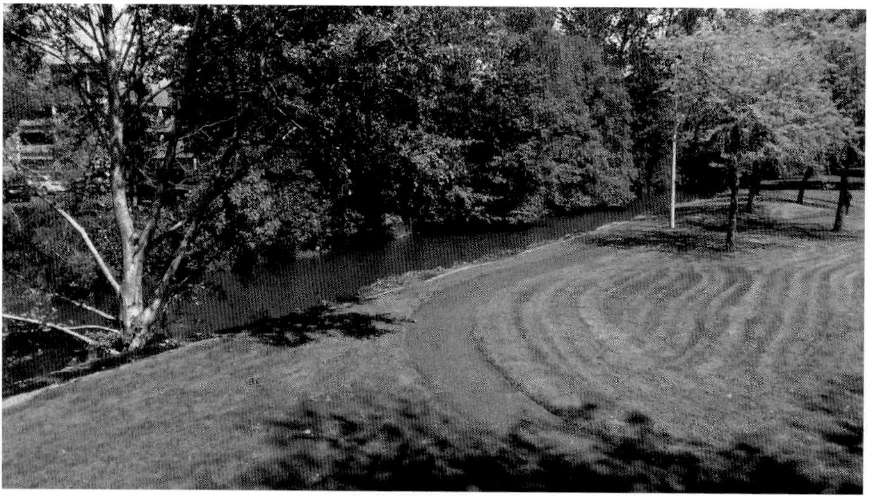

Salem's former hanging ground at today's Pringle Park. *Photo by Tim King.*

In the early years of Salem, justice at the end of a rope was the final solution for several men convicted of murder. Salem's hanging grounds hosted lavish gatherings and used a particular tree, long fallen, to secure the hangman's noose.

Four hangings at the location in today's Pringle Park are documented. They took place in 1851, 1859 and 1865, when two men were hanged. SalemHistory.net suggests that the first hanging in this historic city was a result of questionable justice and that it "could well have prompted a haunting."

THE HANGING OF WILLIAM KENDALL

Some believe that the spooky feeling the place gives off may be connected to the roaming ghost of William Kendall. A tough and sometimes difficult Missouri frontiersman, William Kendall declared his innocence and never wavered from it. He owned property in Salem and was involved in a long-running dispute with a land tenant named William Hamilton.

Several witnesses saw Kendall with a gun. In the most damning testimony against him, a neighbor said he saw Kendall fire a test shot and head toward the area where Hamilton was located. The neighbor then heard another shot ring out, and people began screaming "murder."

The land dispute came about because Kendall believed that Hamilton had stolen some of his hogs. In truth, the hogs were allowed to roam free, and it was very possible that his missing animals could have wandered off and joined bands of feral hogs. Hamilton and his associates made attempts to calm the brooding feud, but Kendall was having none of it. He also had openly threatened to "put a round" in Hamilton; that fact surely led Kendall to the end of a rope.

Still, he said he was innocent and even lunged forward in an attempt to hang himself before his executioner had a chance.

So it is no surprise that the ghost of William Kendall is said to still be at the hanging ground. He was an angry man but perhaps an innocent one—the murder had no witnesses, and the conviction was largely circumstantial.

Kendall even tried for a change of venue, because he didn't believe he would receive a fair trial in Marion County. His wish was not granted.

THE HANGING OF CHARLES JOHN ROE

He loved his wife, as he did his own soul, and he had killed her to keep anyone else from enjoying her.
—Charles John Roe's statement after slicing his wife's throat as she sat holding their two-year old child in 1859.

Those words were used to describe John Roe (or Rose, according to some accounts) shortly after he slit his wife's throat while she was holding their two-year-old child in her lap. Struggling, gasping for her final breath, the beautiful Angelica Carpentier-Roe stumbled outside of her own front door and died in the streets a few minutes after her throat was sliced open from ear to ear.

It was a horrible crime committed by a man who was of major significance among Oregon's early pioneers. Charles John Roe, as an employee of the famous Hudson Bay Company, first arrived in Oregon in 1834. He was one of only thirty white men living in Oregon in 1838.

Roe's first marriage was conducted by none other than Reverend Jason Lee, known as the first European settler of Salem. But the vicious murder of his second wife in 1859 was too much for this man's longstanding reputation to withstand. His grim deed was deemed an atrocious murder.

Roe was initially defiant, but by the day of his scheduled hanging he was repentant and spoke to the audience gathered to watch him die.

Knowing that at least four men were hanged here, it might be hard to decipher which spirit is which.

To learn more about Oregon's early executions, read *Necktie Parties: A History of Legal Executions in Oregon, 1851–1905* by Diane L. Goeres-Gardner.[7]

A PAIR OF KILLERS HANGED

The two men who were hanged in 1865 were convicted in the notorious murder of Daniel Delaney, who was one of the Willamette Valley's early settlers and one of the first slave owners in Oregon. The family's story is documented in a fascinating book published in 2016, *Rachel's Son, Jackson* by Timothy C. McFetridge.[8] The book recounts the often-harrowing circumstances facing Oregon's early pioneer families.

Delaney was murdered outside of his house by two men who hoped to steal a mass of gold and money. There was also history between these men, as they had come together cross country on the Oregon Trail in 1845. The present owner of the historic Delaney House in Salem, Vicki Woods, explains that animosity between the attackers and Delaney dated all the way back to 1845.

One of the men was a former employee of Delaney's named George Beale. His partner in crime was a man named George Baker.

The two men painted their faces black, and gunshots rang out around 5:00 p.m. on January 9, 1865. Baker shot Delaney in the chest with a shotgun, and Delaney fell to the ground. Beale then brandished his pistol and shot Delaney two more times.

BOY LIVES TO TELL THE TALE

The shotgun blast almost hit a small mulatto boy named Jackson DeWolf. This lad ran inside and locked the house, but the two killers blasted their way in, shooting at him several times. DeWolf miraculously escaped being shot. He ran to the home of David Delaney, Daniel Delaney's son, to report what had happened.

Jackson DeWolf would later identify the men and relate his story to a judge. His words led Beale and Baker to the hanging ground in Salem, where thousands gathered to watch them die.[9]

Author Sarah Hunt wrote about Beale and Baker in *Book of Remembrance of Marion County Pioneers, 1840–1860*, published in 1927 and cited by the website marioncountycemetery.com. Beale and Baker had befriended Daniel Delaney, accepting his kindness and willingness to have them stay overnight. In return, the men "plotted and carried out this fiendish scheme."[10]

The two were sentenced to hang by Judge Boise on May 17, 1865. Thousands came to witness the grisly spectacle. Families brought their children from all over Marion County, as well as Polk County and Linn County. Many people were so eager to witness the double hanging that they walked for miles to be in attendance. Friends of Beale and barflies who drank with him came to watch their friend die. It was a day that would be talked about for years, and still is.

Today, the notorious hanging ground is tranquil, beautiful and serene. It is hard to imagine it being a place of death. Yet, a feeling lingers.

JUSTICE OMITTED IN 1885 HANGING

The hanging grounds were the chosen site of execution in the 1850s and '60s, but things changed as years passed. An 1885 hanging in Salem took place at the courthouse.

Knowing that a small African American boy was used to convict the killers of Delaney in 1865, the final hanging in Salem was a step back from progress. On March 20, 1885, an African American man named Joe Drake was convicted in the murder of a man named Dave Swartz and sentenced to hang at the Marion County Courthouse.

Many believed Drake was not guilty of the crime and that he was simply in the wrong place at the wrong time. Nobody stepped forward to help. The killer surely was relieved that an innocent man would take the fall for the crime.

As I have related many times to the horror of those attending my weekend ghost tours, Joe Drake was hanged at the courthouse, on a gallows, and a special barrier wall was erected to prevent the hanging from becoming a public spectacle. But at the last moment, officials decided to allow people into the upper floor of the courthouse and witness the agonizing hanging death of Drake who, in all likelihood, was innocent.

SALEM'S LARGEST MULTIPLE HANGING

The same year that Lucy Jellison murdered four of her children, Salem executed four men who were convicted of murder on December 13, 1912. Each of the condemned men hailed from a different county; their executions had been slow in coming because Governor Oswald West was against capital punishment. In fact, he was so politically averse to the idea that he had proposed abolishing slavery in the previous year's election.

But his idea failed with voters, so Governor West ordered the execution of the four men. A fifth man was condemned to die, but the governor commuted the death penalty in his case.

It is said that the hanging of four men in a single event emboldened West, who continued his campaign to end the death penalty. His wishes were achieved by 1915, when the death penalty was abolished in Oregon. However, just five years later, in 1920, it was reinstated.

In all fairness, Salem was sometimes violent, but not to the extent of many cities and towns in the same time period.

4

Lingering Spirits of the Insane

In the early years it was called, quite unapologetically, the Oregon Asylum for the Insane. Here, tragedy was a daily pattern.

Historians say the State of Oregon was one of the founding parties in the development of eugenics. Lobotomies, shock treatments and the worst of early experimental and largely ineffective treatments were not only administered at the Oregon State Hospital but also were, in part, developed here.

Among the vast indignities that people suffered in their lives was the recent discovery of the remains of hundreds of patients who had died, were later exhumed and had their remains placed on a shelf.

One story brings to mind the lost dead of the Oregon State Hospital. To this day, it is suspected that a large unmarked grave could still exist on the hospital grounds. The problem is that it was either never recorded or the records were simply lost over the years.

That saga relates the story of a young woman named Eva York who died in a bathtub at the Oregon Asylum for the Insane in 1896. Her remains were believed to be located in the copper urns in the hospital's "cremains room."[11]

The *Oregonian* wrote in 2005, "If Eva York is a symbol of Oregon neglect, the hospital itself, its physical hulk is a full-blown metaphor. The tub that she died in is still there, gathering mold and rat droppings in an abandoned wing that's creepier than any haunted house one might imagine."

One is more than fair to question how a woman could die in a bathtub.

ICY, DEADLY WATER

While the records are scant, a movie shot in Salem, *10 Days in a Madhouse*, may hold the answers. You see, doctors in asylums at the turn of the twentieth century had the idea that if a patient was having problems, they should be submerged in a tub of icy water. This raw form of torture was a horrific form of abuse. In the movie, a woman forced into an icy tub simply dies from the shock and cold.

Though her death was attributed to an epileptic seizure, it seems inevitable that poor Ms. York could have suffered the same fate. According to an inquiry that took place after her death, it was determined that she "was left in a bathtub unattended and drowned."

A thirty-six-year-old Marion County woman at the time of her death, York had been locked inside the facility for the five years preceding her death. She reportedly had a brother in Hubbard, Oregon, but her remains, according to the records, were never claimed.

The reported discovery of remains in 2005 was a chilling indicator of widespread abuse and "treatment," according to the *Oregonian*. "Today the corroding canister containing her ashes sits on a plain pine shelf in what's called the 'Cremains Room' at the 122-year-old Salem institution, now known as the Oregon State Hospital. Eva York is one of about 5,000 patients whose cremains are neatly stacked in that stark, lonely room like cans of paint in a well-stocked hardware store."

It was later revealed that researchers could not find her ashes or any record of her cremation. Everything about this place of suffering is a mystery.

HAUNTINGS CONTINUE

It has been speculated by many over the years that the disturbing state of many of the facility's mental patients somehow amplifies the severity of the hauntings.

Another sad fact is that many of the patients at the state hospital were taken there against their will, and many never left, instead perishing inside the aging complex.

The tunnels that wind underneath Center Street have always held great intrigue.

GHOST OF A CORRECTIONS DIRECTOR

Some believe that Oregon's former head of the department of corrections, Michael Francke, who was murdered at the pinnacle of his year-long investigation of state officials, was taken into an underground tunnel and kept there for several hours prior to his bloody murder.

Francke, who worked in the Dome Building on Center Street in Salem, which had originally been the headquarters for the state hospital, had been working feverishly to complete his investigation of state officials in the criminal and court systems of Oregon and was on the verge of turning his investigation over for prosecution when he reportedly went missing on January 17, 1989.

It was shortly after 6:45 p.m. on that day that Francke's car was found unlocked with the driver's side door open. Many hours later, in the early morning hours of January 18, 1989, Francke's body was found next to the door to his office. State officials, as it turns out, had the director's door re-keyed that very day, preventing him from entering his office to gain safety from his killers. Francke had actually punched through one of the glass panels in his door trying to get inside as he was stabbed to death.

Months later, a low-level drug dealer and petty thief, Frank Gable, was convicted of the murder of Michael Francke. Nobody believed it. From the very beginning of the case, all investigators who looked at it came away believing that Francke had been killed to prevent his release of information that would have brought down numerous officials. The public was told that Gable killed Francke in a robbery attempt, yet they never addressed the several hours during which Francke was missing.

A man named Johnny Crouse confessed to the murder about three months into the investigation. He reportedly knew things he could not have known if he hadn't been there when the murder took place. In spite of his confession, Crouse was never named as a suspect.

The fact that Francke had not been robbed somehow failed to register. Nothing had been taken from his body, including his billfold. Then there is the fact that Gable was literally only two-thirds the size of the murdered Francke.

A federal public defender in Portland who today is working on Gable's behalf said the polygraph testing that occurred was the biggest misuse of polygraphy in national history.[12]

To me, the nagging question is, where was Francke taken and held during the first hours? The answer could be very simple. There is an underground access port very close to where his body was later discovered at the Dome Building.

Many people who are close to the case don't have a second thought. They believe Francke was held in the underground tunnel system. What a terrible few hours those must have been for him.

HAUNTING CONTINUES

The state hospital, which dates to 1883, is rarely quiet. The sounds of doors slamming are not infrequent, nor are the sounds of human beings screaming and moaning in fear in these cold, dark underground tunnels.

Many talk about cold spots. It is believed that cold spots are generated by ghosts trying to manifest and be seen. This is the type of cold spot people frequently discuss existing in other haunted locations. The simple theory is that a ghost requires energy to show themselves to living people. This is exactly why the rooms get cold, and it also explains how the batteries that paranormal investigators typically use can suddenly go dead after just a few images have been recorded.

I was fortunate to be able to access the state hospital tunnels a number of years ago. They are extremely extensive. The cold spots are everywhere in this cold, dank area where people were kept for so many years.

Of course, the Oregon State Hospital gained worldwide fame from the movie starring Jack Nicholson, *One Flew Over the Cuckoo's Nest*. That comedic and harrowing story winds through the mind the way the vast array of tunnel systems creeps through the grounds beneath this aging set of structures.[13]

Even today, chains used to restrain human beings and lash them to the dank and cold walls are found in the underground tunnels.

Stories about ghosts in the old tunnels are rife. Employees of the state hospital still talk about tormented, lifeless spirits clinging to our world and roaming the grounds.

One story related to me by a present-day state hospital nurse is particularly interesting. The woman had just been reassigned to a new ward, and a new patient was transferred to a room on her watch. The newly arrived man was unconscious, but the nurse thought she heard him talk.

"Open the door" were the words she heard so clear.

Even though she knew she was alone in the room with the unconscious man, she asked aloud, "Where are you?"

At that moment, her cellphone rang, but nurses at the state hospital cannot take calls during their shift. Later, after her shift ended, she listened to voice messages; one sounded like a very old man. His words—"I'm behind you"—made her heart skip a beat. She recalled that the call came through when she asked, "Where are you?"

So, the next day, the woman tried the phone and got a recording from a man whose voice sounded like the man's voicemail recording.

Further research led her to a chilly conclusion. The call came from the cellphone that belonged to the man who had died in that hospital room where the new man was located.

5

Mysteries of the Mission Mill

I often tell people, "If you ever meet a Mission Mill employee who doesn't think the place is haunted, get a name."

The old woolen mill in Salem, renamed the Willamette Heritage Center, is seething with energy, and it's easy to get the feeling that you're being watched as you wander through the old facility.

The mill is surrounded by some of the earliest surviving buildings in Salem, including the former home of Salem's most famous pioneer, Methodist missionary Jason Lee.

The Willamette Heritage Center is alive with history, though some of the intensity seems more connected to the dead.

Murder Replay

One gripping story that employees have reported involves the ghost of a young woman running across the famous, picturesque North Bridge.

As the legend goes, the woman was being chased by her husband, who then murdered her on the bridge. The tragic scene, it is said, replays over and over again.

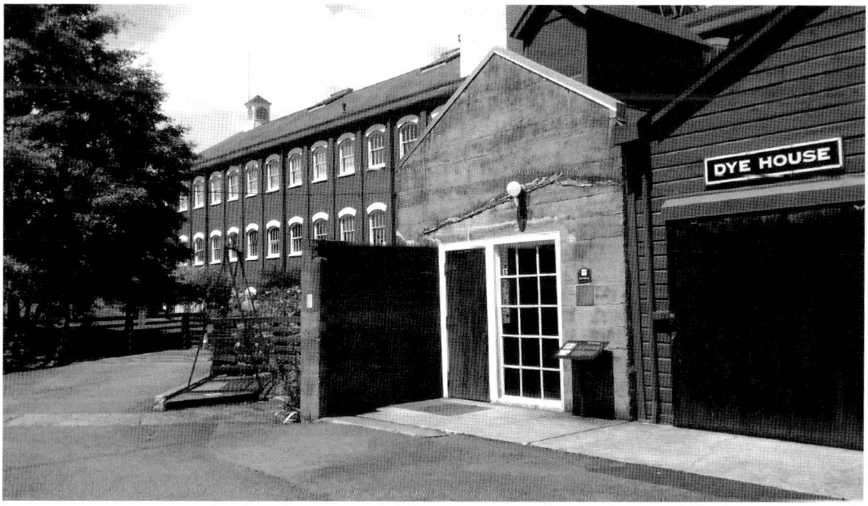

Historic Mission Mill in Salem. *Photo by Tim King.*

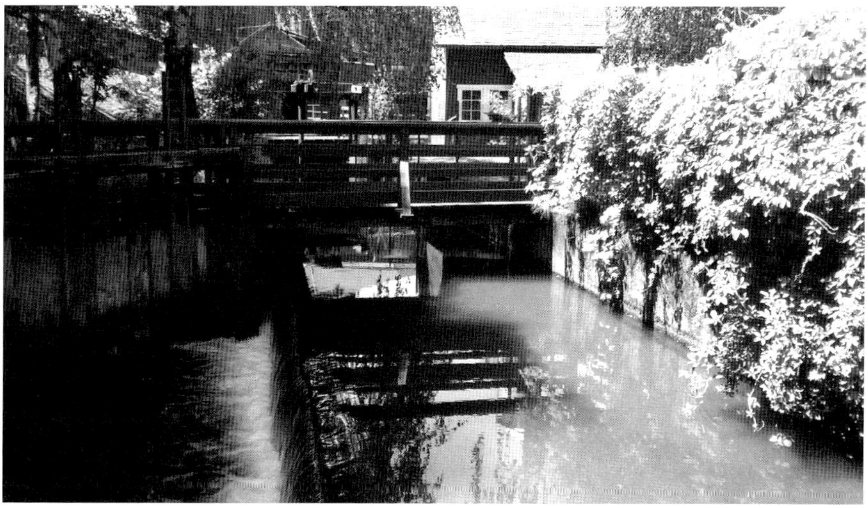

The haunted bridge at the old Mission Mil. *Photo by Tim King.*

Ghost Voices

A Salem ghost investigator once recorded amazing EVPs inside the old woolen mill. EVP (electronic voice phenomenon) is the practice of recording ghost voices, and it dates to the earliest days of audio recording.

Thomas Edison once said in an interview with *The American Magazine*, "I have been at work for some time building an apparatus to see if it is possible for personalities which have left this earth to communicate with us."[14] Shortly after that, Edison was quoted by *Scientific American*: "I have been thinking for some time of a machine or apparatus which could be operated by personalities which have passed on to another existence or sphere."

It is hard to know what Edison really thought about ghost voices, but the quotes cited above suggest that his mind was perhaps already convinced. It is no surprise, then, that the historic Mission Mill's ghosts would fail to remain silent.

The EVPs played for me by one paranormal team were some of the clearest I have ever heard. A woman's voice repeatedly called out, "Help me! Help me!" In a separate recording from the same day, an old man's voice could be heard challenging the paranormal enthusiasts. The chilling words, "Why are you here?" seemed unusually clear.

Other sounds emanate from this place. Vibrations from old machinery that has been silent for years have been heard on many occasions. The thing

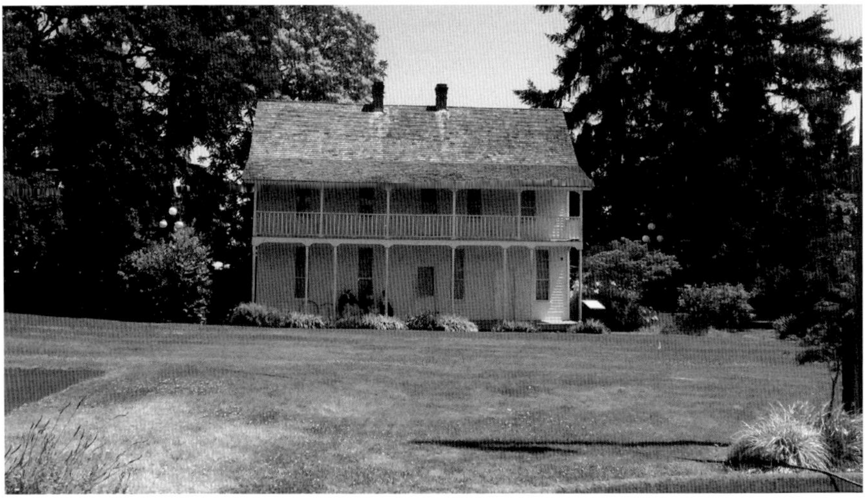

Lonely buildings from the 1850s sometimes host unexplainable voices and sounds. *Photo by Tim King.*

is, the room that housed the machinery is completely empty and is used today for banquets and other affairs.

Another frequently discussed story at the mill involves an old groundskeeper named Wayne who never stopped taking care of the mill's beautiful grounds, even after passing from his mortal existence.

Other lore is even creepier. People sometimes report sensing strong anger and unbearable pain around the old turbine room. Here, it is said, a male employee died a horrible death many years ago.

Visiting the Mission Mill is like stepping back in time. It is one of Salem's most valuable attractions.

6

Strange Saga of a Japanese Celestial

The sad tale of the death of a beautiful woman who lived in Salem in the 1890s, Toyo Watanabe, may be one of the darkest, most passionate in the city's annals.

The building that Toyo lived in—and died in—on Liberty Street in downtown Salem was called the Bell Tower. It was known as a bawdy house, or house of prostitution.

A Senseless Murder

Her vicious murder shocked the residents of Salem, according to accounts in the *Daily Statesman* and *Capital Journal* newspapers.[15]

More than seven years had passed since a murder of great significance and public outcry had left the city reeling. While Toyo's murder remains unsolved to this day, it seems logical that she was probably slain by a jealous lover.

Ms. Watanabe's story is unique. She was a Japanese woman living in a Chinese neighborhood in an American city. Much contrast exists in the accounts of who she was. Most of the writers who covered her murder seemed to agree that she was a celestial—a woman of the night who sold her body to sustain a living. It is noteworthy that some accounts claim that she was married.

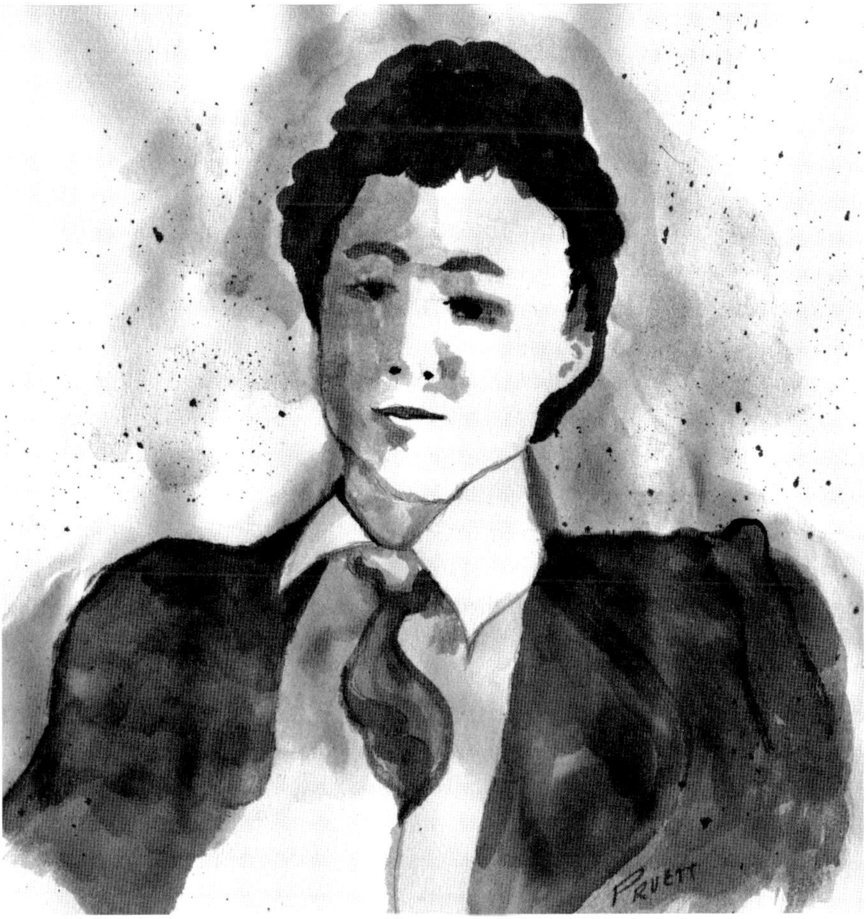

Toyo Watanabe by Shelli Pruett. *Courtesy of Shelli Pruett of North Hollywood, California.*

Even the local newspaper reporters who typically showed disrespect and aimed racist scorn toward the city's Asian population, which was primarily Chinese, were noticeably somber.

DEADLY BOYFRIEND?

It could not have been an easy life for this poor woman from the other side of the world. Somewhere along the way, in Salem, Toyo attracted the attention of a young man who had a checkered past and a wealthy father who always hired lawyers to defend him.

Having the attention of a jealous white man who hailed from a prominent Salem family did not simplify her life. The idea that her ghost still roams the hallway of the city's old brothel paints a sad picture.

The young man who felt strong affection for Toyo was William Hepburn. It is simply too late to really know if he was a suitor, a boyfriend or perhaps simply a john who turned into a stalker.

As the story goes, Toyo and Hepburn were in front of the Bell Tower on Liberty Street, along with a third person, described only as a Chinese man. The three were having a heated discussion that evolved into a screaming match between Hepburn and the Chinese man. Soon a fight developed, and Hepburn grabbed a teapot and hit the Chinese man over the head, knocking him out cold.

A few minutes later, Toyo's horrific screams were heard coming from her apartment in the Bell Tower. By the time she was reached, her throat had been cut three times with a sharp razor. It is said that she lived for an hour

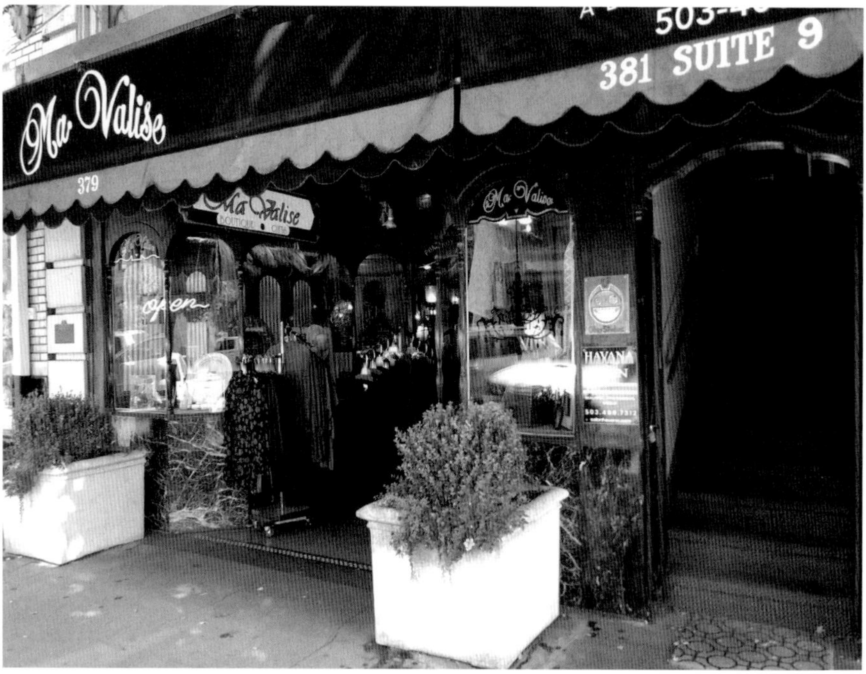

Salem's historic brothel occupied this downtown building for many years. The facility included a dance hall. *Photo by Brittany Anne Dow.*

before expiring. Toyo reportedly nodded her head when asked if she was killed by a Chinese man.

The truth will never be known.

Still Here?

From what I have read, it seems distinctly possible that newspaper reporters were taken up to the deceased woman's room and allowed to see her murdered remains. This would well explain the sympathetic nature of much of what was written by a local press that often openly discriminated against Asian citizens of Salem.

Not far from the old bawdy house is the building that housed Salem's main brothel for many years in the late 1800s and early 1900s. A tattoo artist who rented space in the old brothel related a chilling story of frequent observations of a ghost that he described as an Asian girl who was quite lovely, dressed in very old clothing.

Could it have been Toyo? Is it possible that she worked at different dens of iniquity in Salem besides the Bell Tower?

The story of this young woman whose life was violently stolen continues to draw interest in Oregon's capital city.

7
The Goblin Chuchonnyhoof and Other Native Lore

Long before the Europeans came to Oregon, native people lived here in a peaceful, lush setting. Abundant wildlife and fish kept populations flourishing. In fact, radiocarbon data indicate that human beings have inhabited Oregon for at least 14,300 years.

Native tribes harbored very superstitious belief systems, and their stories caused fear and kept that fear alive among their own people. Perhaps some stories were created to keep children from wandering off and getting lost, but their stories endured the test of time, even if largely lost and forgotten today.

One piece of local lore that never went away comes straight from the tribe that once called the area we know as downtown Salem home. The indigenous Kalapuya tribe talked about a fearsome goblin with an iron hide and sharp claws. That story is said to have terrified children and adults at night when it was discussed around the campfire.

This monster was known as Chuchonnyhoof, said to roam the Willamette Valley looking for unsuspecting and wary travelers, whom it would attack and devour.

In 1995, a woman in Silverton, Oregon, reported seeing a "troll" in her yard. It frightened the woman and her daughter so much that they stayed the night in a motel.[16] Shockingly, the creature is said to have marched back and forth in front of the woman's home. She described it as a "short, hairy thing" according to OregonBigfoot.com.

Of course, the Northwest is no stranger to stories about Bigfoot or Sasquatch, a beast said to roam the forests in this part of the country. It is a cousin to the Yeti, or Abominable Snowman, which is said to exist in the Himalayan region of Nepal, Bhutan and Tibet.

Could the fabled monster of the Kalapuya legend be a Sasquatch? It is an entertaining question. I know people who have personally witnessed a creature that fits the bill perfectly. Of course, where better to turn for Bigfoot data than OregonBigfoot.com? The site maintains a list of sightings, and there have been a number of reported Sasquatch observations in the Salem area.

One story took place in 1996 about thirty miles from Silverton, Oregon, which is about twenty miles east of Salem. A young man was hunting with his father when he was posted on lookout. He spotted an elk, but after only a couple of minutes, the elk took off at a dead run as if sensing something the boy could not.

Then he heard what he described as faint footsteps in the background, and after a moment a creature emerged, which he estimated to be eight feet tall. He said its arms were nearly the length of the creature's body.

He thought he saw a footprint a few hours later, but when he returned in two days to take a casting of it, he could no longer find it. He described the creature as dark brown in color. This witness later contacted a Bigfoot expert in Mount Angel, Oregon, who confirmed that the area is a suspected site for this mythical creature.

Speaking of Mount Angel, in July 2010, a woman who lives on a farm about seven miles northwest of Silverton, in Mount Angel, reported an extremely unusual experience on a warm and clear night. The woman's property is surrounded by open fields and forests in all directions. She says she was sitting outside in her yard when she heard a roaring scream and some type of large animal large crashing through underbrush on the outskirts of the cleared area behind the house.

"I yelled and threw a large piece of firewood in the direction of the scream and whatever it was kept screaming at me for a few more seconds, and then it took off." The woman says there are coyotes and cougars in the area and that she is very familiar with the sounds these creatures make. She said it was not one of those animals.

A reported Sasquatch sighting happened in July 2007 near Detroit, Oregon, about an hour east of Salem, when a father was camping with his children and a few friends and their kids. He says it began with the sound of something big moving near them. The men grabbed their guns and set out to investigate the unusual sounds. The man said, "We saw a silhouette of a large manlike creature in the brush about one hundred feet away from us. We started to follow it but it moved very quickly through the thick brush."

The party circled back to camp. The next day, they found what they described as footprints that were about fourteen inches long and six inches wide. The man telling the story, who is six feet, four inches tall, said he could not begin to reach the distance between the footsteps.

Whatever they saw was massively huge.

The Kalapuya also told stories about a trickster called Coyote, a mythological figure said to have both animal and human traits. With pointed ears and fur, Coyote is depicted as fearless and intrepid. One historic depiction shows Coyote sitting up and rowing a canoe. The stories about this mysterious figure ranged from humorous and mischievous to serious tales of Coyote traveling the land and fighting monsters.

Another mythological creature, known as Amhuluk, was described by the Kalapuya as a sea monster that drowned people in lakes. A story about Amhuluk is found just an hour west of Salem, at a place called Devils Lake, where a sea monster is said to exist to this day.

While those particular stories are absolutely unique to Salem and western Oregon, local tribes including the Kalapuya, whose spiritual belief was known as Spirit or Dream Power, had a realm of other beliefs like other native tribes.

Interestingly, archaeological excavations have shown that as far back as AD 1000 Kalapuya maintained family burial sites or cemeteries. They also left behind hundreds of burial mounds, located along the various rivers in the Willamette Valley.

NATIVE LORE

A commonality among indigenous tribes was a belief in faeries or little people. All across the American continents, native tribes believed in little people. They were distinctly named, and their traits were documented. Some, for example, were believed to be deadly. It is interesting, as a growing number of people today in Salem believe that fairies are real and present.

Native tribes all over the United States and Canada believed in little people. After all, why would this belief system be relegated to Europe? In ancient times, the Celts and others lived very close to nature, exactly like the indigenous peoples of the Americas.

There was the story of a mummy discovered in a cave in Colorado in the 1930s called "The Little Person Mummy," as well as tales about early faeries called "Nimerigar" and "Kwanokasha." There were more almost gang-like little people with names like "Laurels," the "Rocks" and the "Dogwoods." These last three come from the Cherokee tribe. You get the idea that the foggy forests of Europe are far from the only places that faeries are believed to exist. One thing is certain: the way life ended for most native people was no fairy tale at all.

SETTLER CRUELTY

The customs and beliefs of the local tribes had a hard time being sustained after the European settlers began arriving. Murder and abuse of native people became the order of the day in the 1850s. And it was, according to historical accounts, completely unjustified.

In a document titled "Plea for the Indians," John Beeson, an Englishman who had moved to Oregon many years earlier, offered facts and figures about the 1850s Oregon war against Indian people in a *New York Tribune* article.[17] He wrote about a military response that involved the use of three thousand soldiers specially trained to kill and essentially eliminate indigenous people.

The war was a response to panic and fear brought about by the murder of some twenty white people over a period of years in Oregon. In almost every case, the Indians charged with crimes were taken into custody and dealt with legally.

What happened was so bad, so completely excessive, that soldiers and others who participated in the vengeful slaughter of native people over the murder of some twenty white people, over time, exhibited great amounts of remorse. Today, we would call it post-traumatic stress disorder, or PTSD.

Among other things in his report, Beeson made reference to the ghastly genocidal attacks upon the natives by the arriving pioneers. His words are gut-wrenching even today as he described the atrocities committed against the indigenous population.

It begins with a third-party introduction.

> *The author of this forcible tract is a philanthropic Englishman, who from a long residence in Oregon, has become deeply interested in the fate of the Indians in that locality, while he is also convinced that they have,*

> *suffered signal wrongs at the hands of the white inhabitants. He relates a multiplicity of facts showing the aggressive tendencies of the American settlers, and the provocations received from them by the Indians prior to the recent bloody conflicts. His little work abounds in acts and incidents "Illustrative of the character of the aborigines, and fully sustaining the admirable policy of Penn, under which it is stated by an eminent historian 'not a drop of Quaker blood was ever shed by an Indian.'"*

The main epidemics that devastated the Native American population with sickness and disease began in 1829 and lasted until approximately 1850.

An annotation by John Minto, a founding pioneer of Salem, accompanied his 1874 editorial published by the *Willamette Valley Newspaper*.[18] He wrote about a conversation he had with a native man who recalled the terrible years during which so many Indians people perished from from white man diseases.

> *In former conversations George has told me that when a boy he was at the falls of the Willamette during the prevalence of the cold sickness; that the sick were so numerous that many would jump from the sweat houses into the river, die in the water and float away down stream, no attempt being made to take them out for burial. It scarcely needed my knowledge of Chinook to understand the nature of the reply so full of pathos was the tone of the answer. She spoke in particular of the death of a little boy as making her heart very sad.*

After being attacked and sickened with diseases for which they had no immunity, native people were driven away and sent to reservations.

You can wander the trails along Mill Creek where the original inhabitants once lived in Salem and feel the history of this place.

8
More Educated Apparitions

Willamette University in Salem is the oldest institution of higher learning on the entire West Coast.

People on my ghost tours are often surprised that there isn't an older college anywhere in Washington, Oregon or California, but it is true.

At the time of this writing, the university is celebrating its 175th anniversary.

I relate several stories about Willamette on my weekend ghost tours. The place is very old, and this is quite noticeable in the school's earliest buildings, where any person six feet tall has to duck when passing doorways, which also are very narrow, in comparison to anything you would see in a school today.

Poltergeist in the Attic

One of the haunted stories about Willamette involves a dormitory known as Lausanne Hall. The story most people know is that maintenance crews have reported seeing the ghost of a girl in the attic.

What I learned through a former student who lived there while attending the university is that Lausanne Hall is vivid with sounds late at night that are believed to be made by a poltergeist in the attic, who presumably is the girl maintenance crews working in the attic have reported seeing.

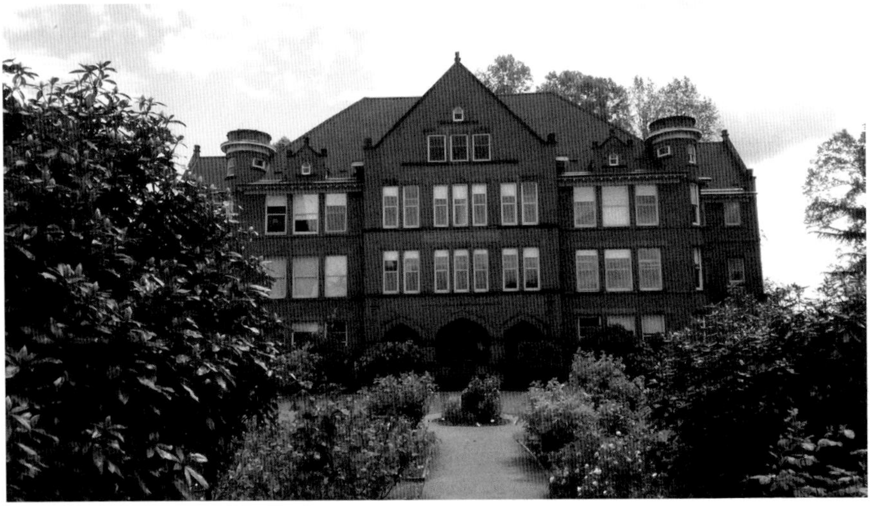

Willamette University in Salem. *Photo by Tim King.*

The German word *poltergeist* means "noisy ghost." The spirit that roams the attic at Lausanne Hall is said to be very aggressive, including creating knocking and banging sounds. It is said to be excessively loud.

The former student I interviewed moved out over it. More than anything, she found herself unable to get adequate sleep. She told me that by the time she decided to relocate, she was more irritated than scared by the ghost in the attic.

GHOSTLY SADNESS

Another female dorm at Willamette, not far from Lausanne, carries a darker story. A Salem attorney who still practices law in the Capital City studied law at Willamette in the early 1960s. She related a story that was incredibly sad, about a night all of the girls in her dorm were getting ready to spend a Saturday night out on the town.

One of the girls wasn't feeling well that night. No one had any idea that this eighteen-year-old was suffering from a life-threatening condition. The girls went out for the evening, and when they returned, their friend had passed away in her sleep.

A highly achieving young woman with a promising future had her life slip away. She then began her existence as an earthbound, intelligent ghost. I often tell people that the best example of an intelligent ghost is found in the movie *Ghost* with Patrick Swayze and Demi Moore.

When a person dies, they see what is described as a white light. This is the exit point, and people are supposed to follow the white light. If they fail to do this, they risk becoming an earthbound spirit.

My suggestions about passing from this life come from the study of near-death experiences. People experience the same thing regardless of their religious or cultural beliefs. I studied and compared notes about EVPs while covering both the war in Afghanistan (2006–07) and the Iraq War (2008). I can tell you conclusively that the white-light theory is universal. The same information is reported by people regardless of their background.

MORE UNIVERSITY SPIRITS

But I digress....Willamette is reported to be the afterlife home of a burglar who was observed trying to break into one of the university's early building's upper-floor windows. Students saw the man and called the police. When they arrived, the officers startled the would-be burglar. He fell to earth, dying on impact.

This spirit is said to cause plenty of trouble by taking items from the maintenance area and returning them hours later. Another poltergeist, this poor soul, as well as others, seems to enjoy simply punking people. Who knew?

9

Who Still Roams the Old Opera House?

I tell people without hesitation that the spirits inside Salem's old opera house are the most intriguing and diverse that I have ever encountered. They are ample and active, and some of the stories of ghosts date to the earlier years of the building, in the late 1800s.

Apparitions show themselves in a variety of ways. Most famous at this location is the "torso ghost," which involves a head and a body but no arms or legs.

The man who built the immense brick structure, a former Civil War general named Cyrus Reed, has reportedly been seen for decades in his military uniform, greeting people and welcoming them to the building before disappearing. Similar stories tell of a striking woman in a red dress. Like the general, she welcomes guests and then disappears. Like the general, she is noted for her armless and legless appearance.

Few buildings stand the test of time the way Salem's old opera house has. When initially constructed and opened in 1870, the opera house, with its massive ceilings and grand architecture, sat 1,500 people, even though Salem only had 1,200 residents.

The stories about ghosts on the second floor, the site of the old theater, abound. People talk about a pair of poltergeists that cause endless mischief. They are believed to be the spirits of two teenage boys who, in the early years of the theater, learned to draw a reaction from the audience with their vaudevillian antics. They enjoy hiding items that the maintenance crews are searching for.

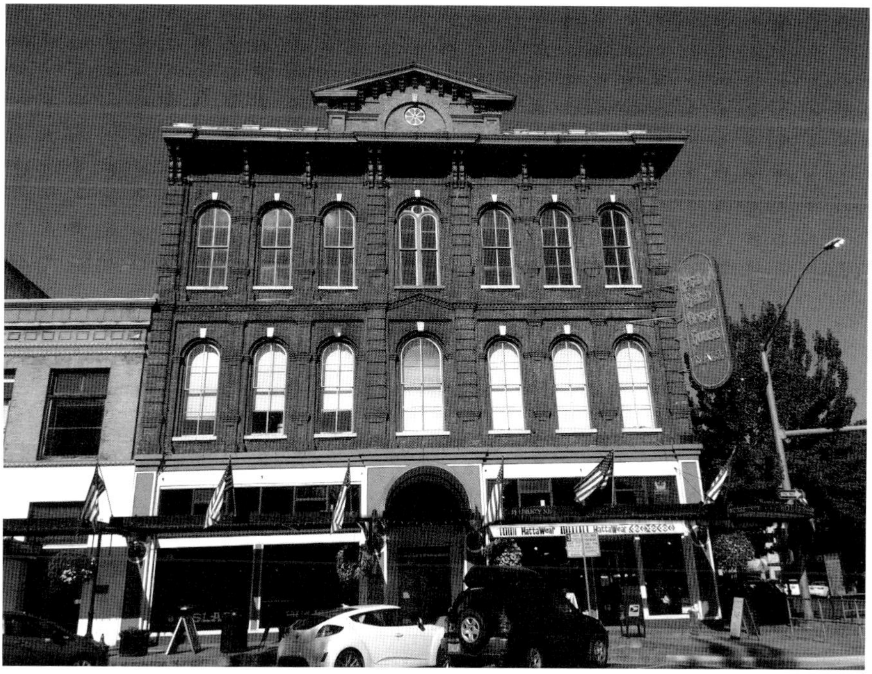

A front view of Salem's historic Reed Opera House. *Photo by Brittany Anne Dow.*

SHADOWY VISITOR

Today, the second floor of the three-story building (four, if you count the underground) is probably the most active. A shadow figure of a man who reportedly wears a top hat is the topic of regular discussion among the councilors who primarily occupy the floor. The shadow man is disturbing, though the figure does not approach people.

Poltergeists run rampant through the old building. The stories are endless. One woman who rented a space and sold Czechoslovakian dolls would close her shop each night, only to return the following day and find the dolls she left displayed in the window completely rearranged. Day after day, this disturbing pattern continued, until the woman decided to literally tape the dolls into place. The next morning, when she opened her shop, they had been rearranged again. She moved out shortly afterward.

Another former tenant had a similar experience. Every night before closing her business, she straightened the throw rugs in her space and made

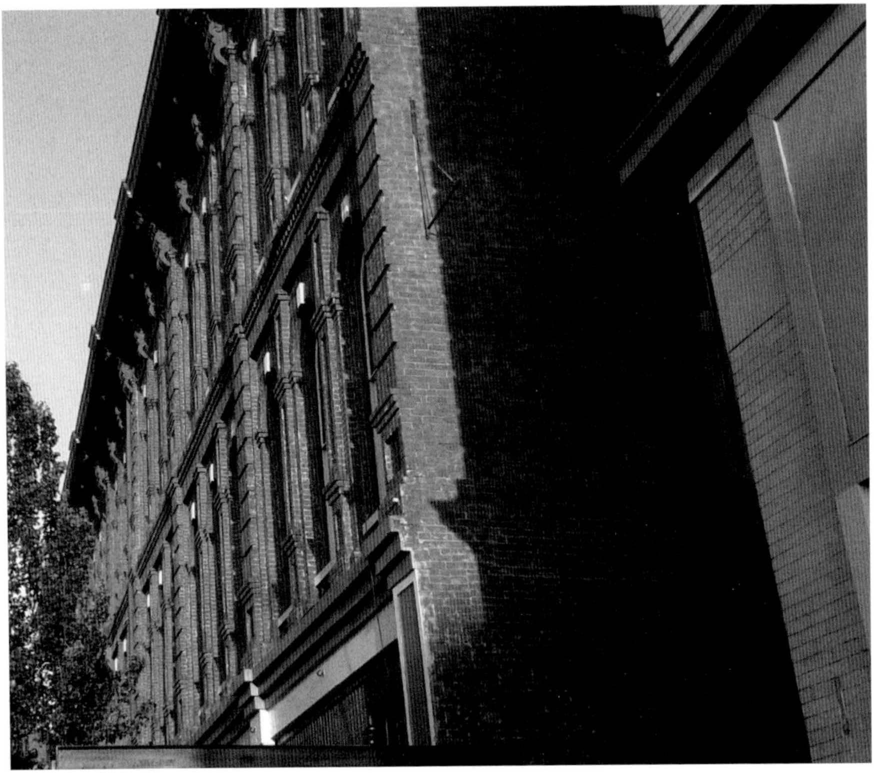

Reed Opera House. *Photo by Tim King.*

sure the place looked tidy. Every morning, she would open the store to find the rugs thrown in heaps. That particular tenant found the experience a bit of a hassle but also saw the humor in it.

A Voice from the Dead

One of the more celebrated historical figures associated with the opera house is the singer Hallie Parish.

They say she sang as lovely as she looked. Adorned in form-fitting dresses made from seal skin, Hallie aged as the building went through its early years, but she is still heard today when the place is quiet.

It was reported that men, including former U.S. presidents Ulysses S. Grant and William McKinley (the latter lived in Salem as a boy) had tears flowing down their cheeks as Hallie sang. She had no rivals. Today, a Salem elementary school is named for her family. People who frequent the old opera house say she never, in fact, left the building.

Under the opera house, the underground tunnels and passageways have been mostly filled in by the city, to many historians' chagrin. Permanently sealed away and blocked off, the underground tunnels held immense history.

Unfortunately, this is the story throughout much of Salem. The tunnels around the opera house were considered some of the city's most historic. The underground section of the building is booming today, and that area has endless stories that cannot in any way be explained.

FLOATING BOY

While reading through interviews conducted more than a decade ago with opera house merchants, I had to raise an eyebrow when reading about the floating boy in the underground.

Witnessed on a regular basis by one merchant, the boy is described as overweight and wearing a uniform that resembles that of Napoleon. The boy floats a few inches above the ground and leans forward, moving slowly along without moving his feet. This is a particularly scary sight according to the former merchant, who eventually adjusted to the otherworldly happenings in the old building.

A unique aspect of the opera house is found in the reports of people dancing in the ballroom at night when the place is locked up tight as a drum. This has been taking place for a very long time at the opera house. Many people report seeing a man in what appears to be a Civil War uniform, dancing with a young woman who is wearing a beautiful nineteenth-century dress. There is never a good explanation; in each event there was no activity in the ballroom.

For decades, people who rode in the elevator at the opera house talked about hearing phantom music while riding between the floors. After many years of this taking place, the music ceased after the carpet in the elevator was replaced. It is all highly illogical; nobody in the building has the slightest idea what the connection between the carpet and the music may have been.

But the spirits of the opera house, regardless of how mysterious and cunning, seem to have a real sense of decency.

In recent years, the fire alarm for the building began sounding, but it sounded distinctly *different* from the alarm that had been installed. Crews arrived and set out to address the potentially serious problem but found the main alarm system idle; it had not been activated. Yet the alarm sound continued. It was described as an old-sounding alarm, like something that might have been installed in the building in the 1930s or '40s.

The search for the mysterious sound continued, finally leading workers to a particular area. When an access panel was opened, faulty wiring was discovered in immediate view. It was extremely serious, and a repairman later said that it could have caused a fire in the old building.

The most bizarre part? As soon as the faulty wiring, on the verge of disaster, was located, the old-time alarm went silent and has never been heard again. Nobody ever figured out where it was coming from.

Were the spirits so dialed in that they literally created their own alarm? Did an old system that nobody knows about today coincidentally just activate and then mysteriously go quiet as soon as the serious wiring problem was found? We will never know, but it seems there are more than just good employees keeping the opera house safe. Indeed, it seems to be a joint effort between the building's living and nonliving admirers.

DON'T DENY THESE GHOSTS

One problem seems to be that the ghosts of the opera house do not like being denied—and why should they see it any differently?

It is not unusual for items to fall off shelves or off the walls when people begin to talk about the place *not* being haunted.

The most famous story, which numerous Salem teens can attest to, involved a tour for children in recent years in an art gallery inside the building, where ancient and historic paintings are displayed. The children asked their tour guide to talk about the "ghosts" and "ghost stories." The tour guide promptly explained that these do not exist in the building.

"We don't believe the opera house is haunted at all" was the first sentence that seemed to cause a professionally hung painting directly behind the guide to be knocked to the floor.

The children drew in their breaths all at once. "Whoa," several exclaimed.

The guide, quick to react, said, "Now if that was a ghost, don't you guys think another painting would fall?"

To the guide's shock and surprise, the very next painting fell to the floor. I want to emphasize that the opera house at the time contained one of the top art collections on the entire West Coast. No paintings in these galleries are hung quickly or shoddily. That event made believers out of a batch of Salem youngsters, and they likely will never forget what they witnessed that day.

HAUNTED DRESSING ROOM

If a person was unkind in their mortal life, it is unlikely that they would suddenly lose that quality when they die and become a ghost.

A story about Salem's old opera house involves the former dressing room of the once-famous Salem singer Hallie Parish. While most people in the building readily agree that her voice, which thrilled audiences in the 1800s, is still commonly heard, almost all seem to find it a positive aspect of the building and appreciate the presence of a person whose career as a singer began when the opera house was opened.

One man who rented Parish's old dressing room as an office was a local private detective. From the moment he moved into the space, he felt what he described as a negative, haunting presence. The man said that the window

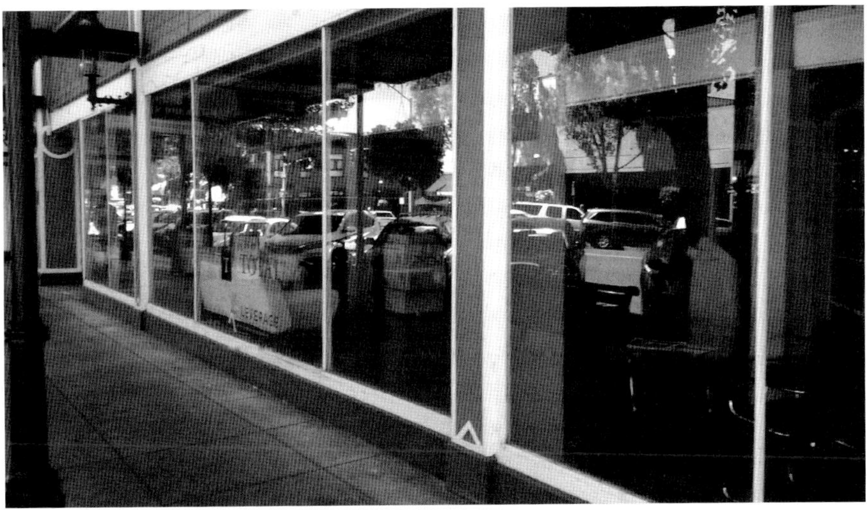

Sounds of a past owner rattle these windows more than 140 years later. *Photo by Tim King.*

shutters, which are opened and closed by twisting a long rod, would begin opening and closing very fast with no assistance from any human being.

He claimed that this disturbance happened only when he was by himself, and that the room was settled and normal as long as he wasn't the only person in the room. Needless to say, the man moved out shortly after.

Another interesting story of the opera house is said to involve the spirit of a man who once owned a grocery store located at street level in the building's earliest days. The man had a habit of tapping his cane on the store's windows as he arrived each morning at 9:00 a.m. to signal his arrival. This allowed his employees to appear busy as he passed through the door to begin his workday. To this day, those who rent the old grocery store space report hearing knocking on the windows each morning at 9:00 a.m.

10

The Profound Behavior of Poltergeists

I would use the word *mischievous* before any other when referring to the behavior of poltergeists, or "noisy ghosts." Based on everything I know, the poltergeist is essentially a more advanced ghost. They have been dead longer and have developed the ability to manipulate objects in our physical world.

They sometimes exhibit tendencies that could be interpreted as mischievous. If a door opens and closes by a ghostly presence, they aren't doing it to pass through the door—they don't need to. They are doing it for another reason, such as to confound and possibly startle or scare a living human being.

Some of the more basic behavior of poltergeists includes turning lights off or on. They seem to love hiding things. Unfortunately for those who coexist with poltergeists, this can be a problem.

I remember a story about a man who worked as a maintenance employee at a historic Salem property. He frequently had tools go missing, only to find them later in the exact spot they had been left.

This same maintenance man told me that he eventually learned to reason with this spirit by explaining out loud that he needed his tape measure because he had to measure a door due for replacement. He would leave the area for a few minutes. Almost always, when he approached the problem this way, his missing item would rematerialize much more quickly.

Can Ghosts and Poltergeists Be Dangerous?

What poltergeists strive to accomplish we will never know, at least while we remain in mortal form. But it seems clear that they tend to operate in mysterious ways for the sake of entertainment.

I am often asked if a ghost can be dangerous. I have never heard of a dangerous ghost, contrary to much popular media. However, it is important to remember that not everything that goes bump in the night is necessarily a ghost. I used to work for an AM radio station that was located in an old haunted building.

There were no employees who started the broadcast day in the morning who didn't later report seeing anomalies, generally out of their periphery.

I had this same experience day after day as the station's news director. I arrived at zero dark thirty and was the first to light the transmitter and begin the day's broadcast. When I finally brought up the anomalies, the station's program director told me this had been going on for years.

Spirits of Persistence

Some time later, I returned to Oregon after spending a few years covering news in Yuma, Arizona, and Las Vegas, Nevada. I was curious about the old station. When I returned to the building, I learned that the radio station had relocated and a Catholic day center for disabled people was using the space.

I engaged the employees in conversation, and when I asked if they ever experienced anything strange, they all reacted intensely, telling me about myriad things taking place for which there was no logical explanation.

One young lady told me that just an hour before I arrived she had entered the supply room, only to have a stapler fly across the small room, right past her face. This is not good. This is not the kind of place that, in my opinion, is simply haunted. There are spirits in our world that are believed to evolve from an evil source, hence the term, "evil spirit," and this idea is not to be taken lightly. Many seasoned paranormal investigators encounter matter similar to this in their endeavors, and the majority choose to have nothing to do with entities of this nature.

In spite of this account, I do not know of any instances of poltergeists actually hurting a person.

11
PHANTOMS OF FAIRVIEW

The "Fairview Home for the Feeble Minded," as it was originally called, easily competes as one of Salem's most haunted places.

Until recently, the buildings of this place stood empty, shutters blowing in the wind, hammering out an awkward rhythm that really seems in tune with the offbeat nature of this place, especially as it exists as a testament to its own shadowy past.

Now, after sitting mostly dormant since the 1980s (the last patient was released in 2000), the buildings are coming down, making way for new inhabitants who will use the land and grounds once dedicated to helping people who were mentally and physically disabled and handicapped.

The stories about Fairview's past are chilling.

I always remind people on my ghost tours that good people worked in these buildings, just as they did at the house of horrors known as Oregon State Hospital.

MENTAL HEALTH, EUGENICS AND GHOSTS

Different eras had different practices, and some were unreasonably cruel and inhumane, even murderous. But toward the end, when former U.S. president Ronald Reagan eliminated much funding that was used to take care of disabled people, the practices had become quite humane. Many in Salem's sizable homeless community are former residents of Fairview.

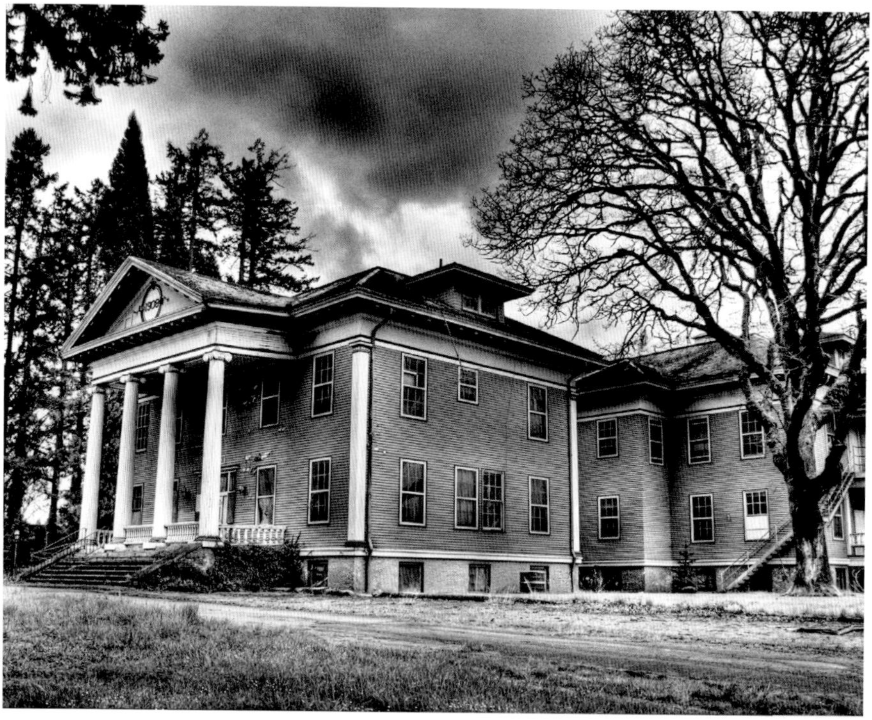

Originally called "Fairview Home for the Feeble Minded," this abandoned institution is a part of Salem's past. *Image by Randy Flook.*

So why would Fairview be considered one of the most haunted locations in a city full of haunted places? In truth, it is the tragic abuse that people suffered. In the beginning, Fairview's patients were called "inmates."

That degrading word set the tone for a zero-tolerance environment. Over time, more than 2,500 forced sterilizations took place. In addition, according to research conducted by the *Oregonian*, "forced hysterectomies, tubal ligations, vasectomies and even castrations were requirements for discharge from Fairview up through the late 1970s."

Governor Calls Out Past Human Rights Violations

In 2002, former Oregon governor John Kitzhaber called the acts human rights violations and offered a formal apology.[19]

There were stories about girls being tied to beds and burned with boiling water as punishment for breaking rules. Leather cuffs, cow whips, razor straps and isolation cages are all part of Fairview's past.

Seven days a week, the "inmates" were forced to get up at 5:30 a.m. and often were forced to work in jobs throughout the day.

Fairview as a Movie Set

Fairview and the old buildings there were used in a 2015 movie recorded in Salem called *10 Days in a Madhouse*.[20] The film's story followed the incredible journey of an investigative journalist named Nellie Bly, who posed as a mental patient in order to infiltrate a mental facility for women on Blackwell's Island off of New York City.

Working covertly for Joseph Pulitzer, Bly succeeded in documenting the deadly abuse and emerging after ten days to write her stories. The journalism not only closed the facility on Rockwell Island but also saw it razed to the ground.

I spent a bit of time on one of the movie's sets and came to know the creator, Tim Hines, and his family, actors and crew. Many related creepy stories about things they saw during the filming at Fairview. Doors slammed shut, disembodied voices were frequently heard and objects were sometimes tossed about by unseen hands.

The place just seems to hold or possess the spirit that loomed over people here, making them alone and fearful and often in pain over their own physical and mental shortcomings.

One thing about Fairview: even though it is closed and posted with "No Trespassing" signs, there is no lack of traffic from Salem kids and people from other places, who, without authorization, enjoy the sport of urban exploration (UE). Others get permission to visit the place, like the movie company I referenced, and the Salem Oregon Paranormal Society, which visited the Fairview Training Center for an investigation. Its members reported hearing audible voices, recording EVPs and shooting photos of orbs—silver and grayish round anomalies that often show up in photographs taken in haunted locations.

On my ghost tours, I explain that, in my opinion, the orb is the entry-level manifestation of a ghost. Frequently recorded in snapshots, orbs are sometimes visible in recorded video.

As a reporter/photojournalist for KATU Channel 2 News in Portland, my former employer, I followed the story of a paranormal investigation team that brought their work home with them, for lack of a better phrase. They recorded orbs on video on their flight of stairs for no less than forty-five minutes. I took that video, had it analyzed and verified the fact that the video was not enhanced. That report captivated viewers and sat on the front page of KATU.com for months. People voted whether or not it was a real ghost.

Fairview's ghosts are, by most accounts, quite real.

One phantom of Fairview is described as an old woman who seems to patrol the grounds of the old institution. This woman's form has been observed in the late hours of the night, as has another ghost who appears near one of the school's many cottages.

HAUNTED COTTAGES

SalemHistory.net references Holderness Cottage, which housed the more aggressive patients at Fairview, as another place where restless spirits roam the grounds. A former employee reportedly saw the ghost of a man in his thirties on three separate occasions walking through doors without unlocking them first.

Among many spectacular reports about underground tunnels spanning all the way from Fairview to the equally haunted (according to many reports) nearby Hillcrest School are reports of dozens of bodies once kept in a cemetery that nobody today seems to have any record of. It is not known if the gravestones were simply removed, or if the bodies were re-interred somewhere else.

Perhaps the saddest and most documented haunting at Fairview is that of the the ghost of a small boy, a student named Hollie Pollock who went missing in November 1923 and then, shockingly, began to show up in the most terrible way: his hair and skin particles began to flow through the school's water pipes.

Three weeks after going missing, the lad's decomposing body was found in the well.

I've seen a person who had drowned in fresh water and was retrieved three weeks later. He was three times the size of the man that went into the water. Hundreds of pounds of water had been absorbed into the man's corpse. Pulling the boy out of the well could not have been an easy thing to do. It was a very sad event indeed.

The boy's death was deemed a drowning, presumably accidental, but it does seem fair to ask the question, Why would he climb into a well and drown himself when he could easily just leave? The authorities said they thought he had run away. It seems distinctly possible that the poor boy was murdered and his body dumped in the well.

The old well or cistern has long since been covered, though many believe the ghost of Hollie Pollock still dwells nearby.

12

Riverfront Revenants

Very few homeless residents will tell you the riverfront of Salem is quiet at night. There are periods of quiet, of course, but those moments are frequently shattered by a howling moan or distant scream.

The spirits of native warriors and hunters still navigate along the paths, murmuring in languages that are totally unrecognizable and all but forgotten. More modern spirits, those of drowning and murder victims, find little rest, as they often harbor near where they took their final breath.

There are the stories you hear and read about, and there are the things you personally witness. The latter group, of course, is generally most impactful, and I feel my skin crawl every time I think about the sounds the river produces at night.

At Minto Brown Island in Salem, you get a real sense of the past. The nine-hundred-acre undeveloped area has trails that wind through what could only be described as peaceful, yet creepy, country. There are old cars from the 1920s through the 1950s that must have been dumped here when there was an actual road rather than trails.

Locals know that this is the place where an eighteen-year-old Salem girl, Sherry Eyerly, disappeared on July 4, 1982.

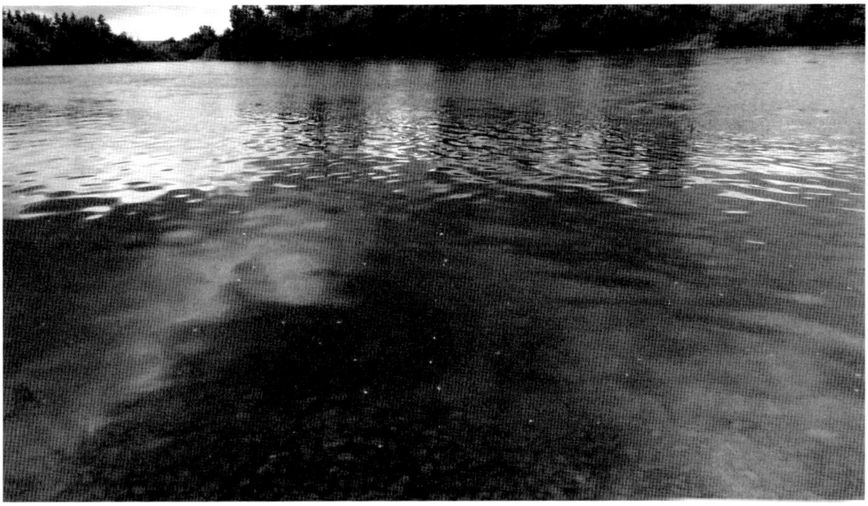

Willamette River. *Photo by Tim King.*

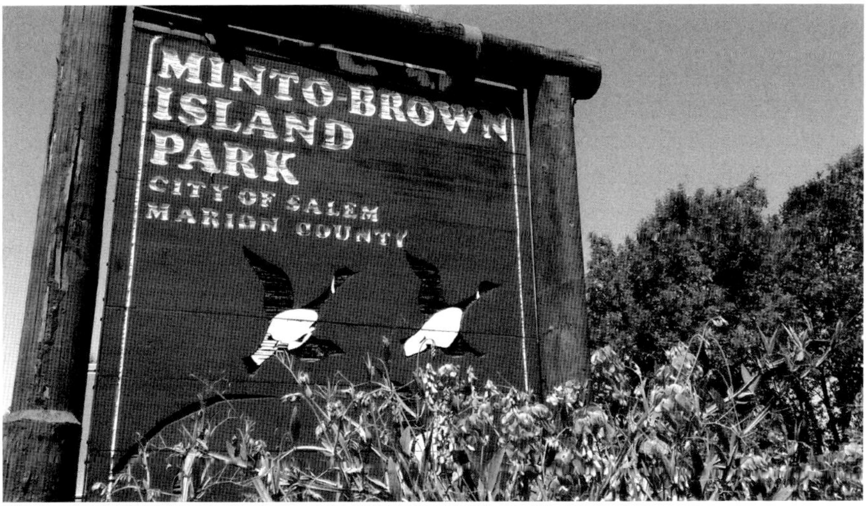

Minto Brown Island Park in Salem. *Photo by Tim King.*

TRAGEDY OF SHERRY EYERLY

Working as a delivery driver for Domino's Pizza, she was called out to Riverhaven Drive South, near Minto Brown Road, to deliver a pizza, and she was never seen again. Eyerly's car door was wide open, her parking brake was set and three large unopened pizza boxes were on the ground.

The order had been placed from a motel room by a person using a false name. The following day, a ransom demand was made, but the demand was never issued again. The family heard nothing more from the suspected kidnapper.

In 2004, while I was an employee of the ABC station in Portland, KATU, I covered a story about how the Marion County Sheriff's Office had formed a cold-case team. Incredibly effective, cold-case teams comprise retired law enforcement officers and officials, and they have tremendous success tracking down the truth when trails go cold.

I interviewed a Marion County homicide detective named Mike Meyer. He told me that Sherry Eyerly's case, which would be solved only three years later, was not being added to the list of cold cases. That made no sense to me, as Eyerly was probably the area's most famous cold case.

Meyer specifically told me not to use Eyerly in the story, and I relayed that information to my producer. Nevertheless, he still used footage of the Eyerly disappearance scene in the story. Meyer never forgave me for that, even though the matter was out of my hands. To this day, I still wonder why on earth her case would have been neglected.

The Charley Project keeps track of missing people. It publishes current information about cases and explains in its article about Sherry Eyerly that a suspect named Darrell J. Wilson committed suicide just one month after her disappearance and only a few hours after police had questioned him about the girl's disappearance.[21]

Wilson initially denied knowing Sherry Eyerly but later told police that she was an acquaintance. He also drove a green pickup truck, similar to a vehicle that had been spotted in the area the night of Eyerly's disappearance.

In the weeks following the disappearance, Wilson painted his pickup brown. He claimed to have been camping at Elkhorn Lake, more than half an hour's drive east of Salem. It was learned that he did go camping, but also that he had left the campsite from 6:30 p.m. on July 4 and had not returned until around 3:30 a.m. the following morning.

It was announced in late 2007 that a man named William Scott Smith had confessed to Eyerly's murder and had entered a guilty plea in the case.

Smith is currently serving two life sentences for the rape and murder of two other Salem women. He claimed to have dumped Eyerly's remains in the Pudding River, but authorities never found a trace of any of the three.

Smith implicated another man in the crime, Roger Noseff, and claimed it was Noseff who made the ransom call. Smith claimed to have strangled Eyerly, who was five feet, two inches tall and weighed one hundred pounds.

Journalists have questioned the validity of Smith's confession. Paranormal investigators claim that Eyerly haunts Minto Brown Island. In no way do I mean to be disrespectful to the family, but I mention it because some extraordinary EVPs believed to be from Eyerly have been recorded.

One recording was made in the shack, a closed cement building that locals suspect to be the location of Eyerly's murder and possibly also the general area where she was buried. The shack is a short distance from the memorial for Sherry Eyerly, which was the scene of her abduction. In that particular EVP, a woman's voice is heard saying, "There's no way out of here!"

In another recording from the Salem Oregon Paranormal Society, a woman named Megan is asking the suspected ghost of Sherry Eyerly questions. As they prepare to stop the recording, a haunting voice slowly says "Megan," as if asking the interviewer to stay.[22]

In my early days of paranormal research in Salem while working for KATU, the place where Sherry Eyerly disappeared was one of the first sites I visited. I took clairvoyant friends there on more than one occasion, and all confirmed that a thick and negative energy surrounded the place. They sensed her fear and confusion, as well as her knowledge that her life was going to come to an end and there was nothing she could do about it.

Some believe Eyerly's ghost is there; others attribute the negativity to other sources, even attributing energies sensed on the island to evil spirits.

It is tragic that the life of this young woman who had recently graduated from Sprague High School in Salem was cut short in such a senseless and cruel crime. If her ghost haunts those woods as many suspect, I hope that someday she will be able to rest in peace.

GHOST SHIP

Few spots in Salem that are off the beaten path have a view of the Willamette River, but one location I frequent, a couple of miles from Salem's downtown, offers a nice view, particularly in fall, when the leaves of the trees and bushes that obscure the river blow away.

It is at this location that I have heard the phantom boat pass. First you feel it, and each time the feeling is the same. It is uncomfortable, and as soon as I take note of that, the sound becomes audible. It isn't an engine sound; it is the sound of the bow of a vessel cutting through the water. It is a creepy sound, and whatever causes it contains mass and size—or so it seems.

What makes it distinctive and most noticeable is the seeming immensity of it. This is no rowboat; it sounds like one of the huge old sternwheelers that endlessly plied the river in the late 1800s.

The creepiest part? Voices…indistinct human voices, hollow-sounding, faint but present. It's like they're drowned out by the sound of the invisible ship's hull slicing through the cold river. It all comes at once, and each time, I strain my eyes staring at the black water trying to see something, *anything*.

DEATH ON THE RIVER

In April 1854, a regular visitor to Salem, the steamship *Gazelle*, had both boilers blow up while docked on the river a number of miles north of Salem.[23] On board were sixty souls; at least twenty were killed instantly, their bodies in some cases blown to pieces. The dead and injured, along with wreckage from the stricken vessel, immediately began floating down the river.

This is one of many deadly shipwrecks and explosions that rocked the communities along the Willamette River. The *Gazelle*'s normal route included daily stops in Salem and Corvallis.

According to the article "Awful Explosion of Steamer Gazelle: Twenty-Eight Lives Lost!!!: Thirty Others Wounded!!" published by the *Oregon Spectator* on April 14, 1854, human body parts were blown in all directions. The remains of people aboard the *Gazelle* were launched into the river and onto the shore, though most of the people killed were found on the forward deck. The article references a man named David D. Page, the chief superintendent of the Willamette Falls Canal, Milling and Transportation Company of Linn City (now West Linn, about eleven miles south of Portland), which owned the ship. Page died instantly. When he was killed, according to the article, his head was "dashed to pieces." He was identified only by his clothing.

13

Prostitute Tragedies and Haunts

Salemites regard the ghost of a smiling woman who is seen around Liberty and State Streets as possibly that of Maggie Gardner, the madam of a Salem brothel, a woman of great notoriety—at least, that's one way to put it. She was one of the first white American women to be married in California, years before she came to Salem in 1867.

She was born in Salem, but not the one in Oregon, Gardner hailed from Salem, New Jersey. She arrived in San Francisco in 1849, literally the only woman present, surrounded by thousands of newly arrived miners.

She had several marriages, one to the sea captain of the vessel she sailed to California in from the East Coast. At one time, the woman known as Maggie Gardner (she had used several names in her lifetime) was said to be worth an estimated $100,000.

She built a seventeen-room hotel in San Francisco called the New York House when the hills of the city were barren, with very few buildings present. Writers with CapitalCityBlogspot verified that the New York Hotel was up and running in 1850.[24]

Maggie Gardner was a unique woman, to say the least. In her years as the madam of Salem's most popular brothel, she had many entanglements with the law. She was looked down upon and scorned by women in particular and drew the wrath of Salem's holier-than-thou socialite set, which believed she represented something undesirable in their city.

The problem for the women who opposed Gardner was that their husbands didn't all have ill will toward the world's oldest profession.

Another important fact is that prostitution in Oregon was legal in the 1800s and early 1900s.

In downtown Salem, people say Maggie Gardner is still present. Her distinguishing quality was that when people looked down upon her or made statements toward her that were unbecoming, she always smiled at them. Whether or not it made a difference is unknown, but a smile can have a positive effect and sometimes even create a positive outcome when used in a difficult moment.

Another tragic story about a prostitute in downtown Salem took place in the late 1800s. It involved a young woman from Denver, Colorado, who had moved to Salem in 1896 at the age of twenty after having a child in Colorado. Her name was Emma Reisner, but she used the name Pauline Phillips.

She was one of the Ferry Street Peppermint Flat girls. It is hard to imagine it today, but Ferry Street had a substantial gathering of brothels in the late nineteenth century. She worked for a madam named Hattie McGinnis.

Phillips met a "sporting" man in Salem with whom she fell in love. The man told her he loved her and would rescue her from her life as a prostitute. Sadly for Pauline, the man visited her one night and told her in no uncertain terms that he was going to break up with her and that he didn't want to see her again.

The young woman began drinking; in her shattered state, she began breaking windows of businesses on State Street. Salem police were called to the scene. They located Pauline in a despondent state. She was sent to the asylum for a period of time and then released into the custody of McGinnis.

CapitalTapsBlogspot offers an extensive review of this woman's life and death. It cites a newspaper article from the time that reads, "Pauline Phillips, an occupant of a house of ill-fame at 142 Ferry Street committed suicide Thursday afternoon by drinking carbolic acid."

It is said that McGinnis and the other prostitutes did what they could, but Pauline Phillips, twenty-four years old, suffered a miserable death, writhing in agony for hours before finally passing. Surely she could have found a better way to take her life than drinking acid, but that was her choice.

As a response to the tragedy, McGinnis hired an elaborate horse-drawn funeral procession and had Pauline placed in the ground at the Pioneer Cemetery. Today, her headstone is knocked over, clearly the work of vandals.

It is a sad story from a time when women had no rights and were treated little better than animals. Salem's residents never really came to terms with the brothels, and eventually those sentiments would criminalize the practice and drive it underground.

14
Oregon State Penitentiary Ghosts

Prisoners at the Oregon State Penitentiary say an inmate walks up and down metal stairs in the prison's D block. The ghost of another prisoner, who reportedly bled to death, somehow has figured out how to commandeer the intercom system. How's that for creepy? Knowing that a ghost is able to make announcements?

Ghosts have been keeping prison guards awake for years at the north tower of the historic Oregon State Prison. Many have talked openly about the haunting presence that has been an active subject at the prison for nearly one hundred years. As it turns out, tower number four is reported to be built squarely atop a prison graveyard that was abandoned in 1917. By 1923, the graveyard was turned into a recreational yard, and the tower was later built in the same location.

Prison guards, or correctional officers as they are referred to today, have long documented the strange things that take place in the tower, particularly on the graveyard shift. They report feeling a presence when they are completely alone.

We all know that Indian gravesites are the last place a person wants to construct a home. The same apparently holds true for this former/current graveyard of obscurity. The simple truth is that the Oregon State Penitentiary has been the scene of a lot of death throughout its existence.

Built in 1851, the prison has always been a rough place. Many escapes in the early years were documented, and some turned deadly. One of the earliest escapes was extremely significant. It happened in August 1866, when a number of prisoners took the superintendent and warden at knifepoint and forced them to open the prison gates, allowing all of the convicts to escape.

Before it was over, one prisoner was wounded by a gunshot, eight of the convicts escaped and a convicted horse thief named George Hibler received a fatal gunshot wound in his jail cell. Hibler was a recently arrived, belligerent and dangerous man, so he was described in reports.

Hibler was a rough character. On one particular day, five men were required to force him out of his cell for a medical examination. Hibler reportedly said he would kill the first man who touched him. He was shot to death by a guard named Charles McNalley, who claimed he shot Hibler in self-defense. A jury inquest didn't buy it, finding the shooting "non-justifiable."

Every few years in the 1800s and early 1900s, the Oregon State Prison was the scene of a significant escape. In July 1883, fourteen prisoners escaped. Four were killed, and one more later died while being recaptured.

A noted escape in the early years of the automobile happened on August 12, 1915, when three armed convicts, Tom Murray, James Willos and Ellsworth Kelly, killed two prison guards and commandeered a taxicab from the state hospital, forcing the driver to take them to Polk County. One prisoner also died during the escape.

As SalemHistory.net cites, the escape and freedom journey of Murray and Willos was short-lived. Both were recaptured within ten days of their violent escape. Kelly had only thirty days left to serve at the time of the escape.

All three were sentenced to hang, but Murray decided to take the job into his own hands. He hanged himself in his cell on May 9, 1925. Kelly and Willos were hanged on April 20, 1928.

In the time following those early, violent and tumultuous years, the prison has seen much death, both from natural causes and homicidal acts. It continues to house dozens of men on death row who are convicted of murder. It seems fitting that such a place would be haunted.

Perhaps one of the reasons prisoners went to such lengths and efforts to escape was the treatment they received at the hands of the staff and guards. According to a book written in 1908 by Joseph "Bunko" Kelly titled *Thirteen Years in Oregon State Penitentiary*, the prison was absolutely brutal.[25] Floggings were a regular occurrence. Kelly noted that race had nothing to do with it—whites, blacks, Indians and a Chinese "half boy and half woman" were abused and received inadequate care from negligent doctors, who also failed to address issues of mental health among the inmates.

Kelly noted a five-year period during which the inmates at the Oregon State Prison were denied access to newspapers. He wrote about how the guards would become intoxicated and that the alcohol abuse led to worse treatment as the guards took their aggression out on the prisoners.

While the prison ended the use of flogging as a punishment in 1904, replacing it with cold water sprayed by a hose, the abuses did continue, even if not as part of institutional norms.

15

1918: The Year of Death

Few years compare to the horrors of the great 1918 influenza, or Spanish flu, outbreak. Of course, the event lasted longer than a year, but 1918 was the worst, as people died in droves all over the world. The U.S. military lost more soldiers to the flu during World War I than in combat. Oregon was no stranger to this terrible outbreak.

Lawrence Broxmeyer, MD, a medical investigator, said of the 1918 event:

> *I heard that seven men dropped dead in a doctor's office after being vaccinated.*[26] *This was in an army camp, so I wrote to the government for verification. They sent me the report of U.S. Secretary of War Henry L. Stimson. The report not only verified the report of the seven who died from the vaccines, but it also stated that there had been 63 deaths and 28,585 cases of hepatitis as a direct result of the yellow fever vaccine during only six months of the war. That was only one of the fourteen to twenty-five shots given the soldiers. We can imagine the damage that all of these shots did to the men.*

Broxmeyer added:

> *All the doctors and people who were living at the time of the 1918 Spanish Influenza epidemic say it was the most terrible disease the world has ever had* [seen]. *Strong men, hale and hearty, one day would be dead the next. The disease had the characteristics of the black death added to typhoid, diphtheria, pneumonia, smallpox, paralysis and all the diseases the people*

> *had been vaccinated with immediately following World War I. Practically the entire population had been injected "seeded" with a dozen or more diseases—or toxic serums. When all those doctor-made diseases started breaking out all at once it was tragic.*

Broxmeyer says the twenty to forty million deaths worldwide from the great 1918 Influenza Pandemic were due not to the flu or a virus, but to pneumonia caused by massive bacterial infection.

As you wander the gorgeous trails that wind along Mill Creek in Salem, you forget you are in a city. The lush foliage is fresh and alive, as the native people were who once thrived in this area. Later, the area around the pond at what is now city hall became the place of residence for Salem's homeless population. The city was very unprepared for the devastating flu symptoms that set in quickly.

With few alternatives, the homeless population of Salem in 1918 began to die off. It is said that so many died so quickly that they had to be buried in paupers' graves. It was a difficult time for those with limited alternatives.

Many who have studied the area around Salem City Hall and Mill Creek for paranormal activity, expecting to research native energies, emerged with EVPs that seem to have possibly come from the immense die-off in 1918.

One tragic fact that may have led to the accelerated spread of the Spanish flu was the fact that the United States had sent so many doctors overseas to the First World War. The physicians who may have helped slow the progress of the flu were gone. Reduced medical care may have been a large contributor to the outbreak, according to the *Bend Bulletin* newspaper.[27]

All told, at least 3,688 people in Oregon died from the outbreak. Between 500,000 and 650,000 Americans died from the disease. As a native woman named Marsha Small discovered while conducting research at the historic school (commonly believed to be haunted), the death toll from influenza at the Chemawa Indian School was outrageous.[28]

As part of her master's thesis research at Montana State University, Small brought a ground-penetrating radar system to the Chemawa Indian School, discovering in the process a number of unmarked graves. She believes there could be hundreds.

Chemawa is one of the few remaining native boarding schools in the United States still in operation. The school lost many students and teachers during the 1918 outbreak.

While the school today builds character and is administered by caring, sensitive people, the early years were horrible, and children at Chemawa died all too frequently. This is a story that was told over and over again throughout both the United States and Canada.

In her thesis, "A Voice for the Children of Chemawa Cemetery," Small revealed her discovery of the unmarked graves. She says practices at the government- and church-operated schools were in keeping with infamous "kill the Indian, save the man" approach.

An Al Jazeera article about Marsha Small from January 3, 2016, quotes Captain Richard H. Pratt, who, after fighting in the Indian wars, started the first Indian boarding school in 1879. His words defined the American attitude toward the nation's indigenous people, saying, "Transfer the savage-born infant to the surroundings of civilisation, and he will grow to possess a civilised language and habit."

Forced assimilation was the order of the day for the Native American population. At the peak (or, perhaps more accurately, the nadir), almost 90 percent of all native children were placed in boarding schools throughout North America. As Small relates, many were forcibly taken from their families, made to convert to Christianity and forced to abandon their native cultural traditions and beliefs.

Tragically, many were victims of extreme, brutal abuse—physical, emotional and sexual. Small said, "Our homelands are the places where we're taught everything, where we go to feel full and heal as indigenous people." Small laments the fate of the unfortunate Indian children forced into this life. "For these children to be buried in an unknown land with an unknown prayer, I can't think of a more horrific fate."

Many children at the Chemawa Indian School died during the influenza outbreak. Many also died from tuberculosis and trachoma, which swept through the school in other years.

But 1918 was different, and poor native children and members of the penniless homeless community are not the only people who fell victim. In fact, one of Salem's premier families lost a daughter to this dreaded threat. Indeed, nobody was completely safe or immune.

One Salem school, McKinley Elementary, became a hospital and a morgue to keep up with the rapidly dying population in 1918.[29] SalemHistory.net explains that the school had an operating room and a kitchen located in the basement. In 1920, McKinley resumed its place as a Salem school, serving as a junior high school. By 1927, it had again become an elementary school.

The school is rumored to be haunted. The source of the haunting is reported to be the 1918 influx of living and dying influenza patients.

16

Other Ghosts of Salem

Salem, Oregon, is no stranger to ghosts, and the stories predate the arrival of European settlers to this land long cherished by indigenous people. Terrible murders, disease, harassment and general eradication programs spelled an end to the existence of many native tribes here.

As white people increasingly moved into the Willamette Valley, the settler ghost stories began to emerge. One area of Salem long known for its haunted atmosphere is the Chemeketa-Court Historic District.

Located a stone's throw from the city's prominent state capital mall, the nineteenth-century houses east of Twelfth Street, on Court and Chemeketa Streets, are replete with stories of ghosts and inexplicable phenomena.

Several of the Victorian homes on Court and Chemeketa date to the 1870s, when many of Salem's downtown businesses were built. These old homes seem to have their own tendencies. Residents of one of the homes have spoken of candles lighting by themselves in the middle of the night.

Other stories tell of poltergeist activity that goes on regularly: windows opening and closing, lights going off and on by themselves and "malevolent energies creating dissension in the adult relationships."[30]

One of the homes is said to have the spirit of an angry man who refuses to leave. These entities and their attributes have sent more than one Salem family fleeing into the night. In one case, a family living in one of the historic haunted houses never returned—not even to collect their belongings!

One home in the historic district has presented a visual replay of an angry Dutch man strangling his wife to death. This is a crime that took place more

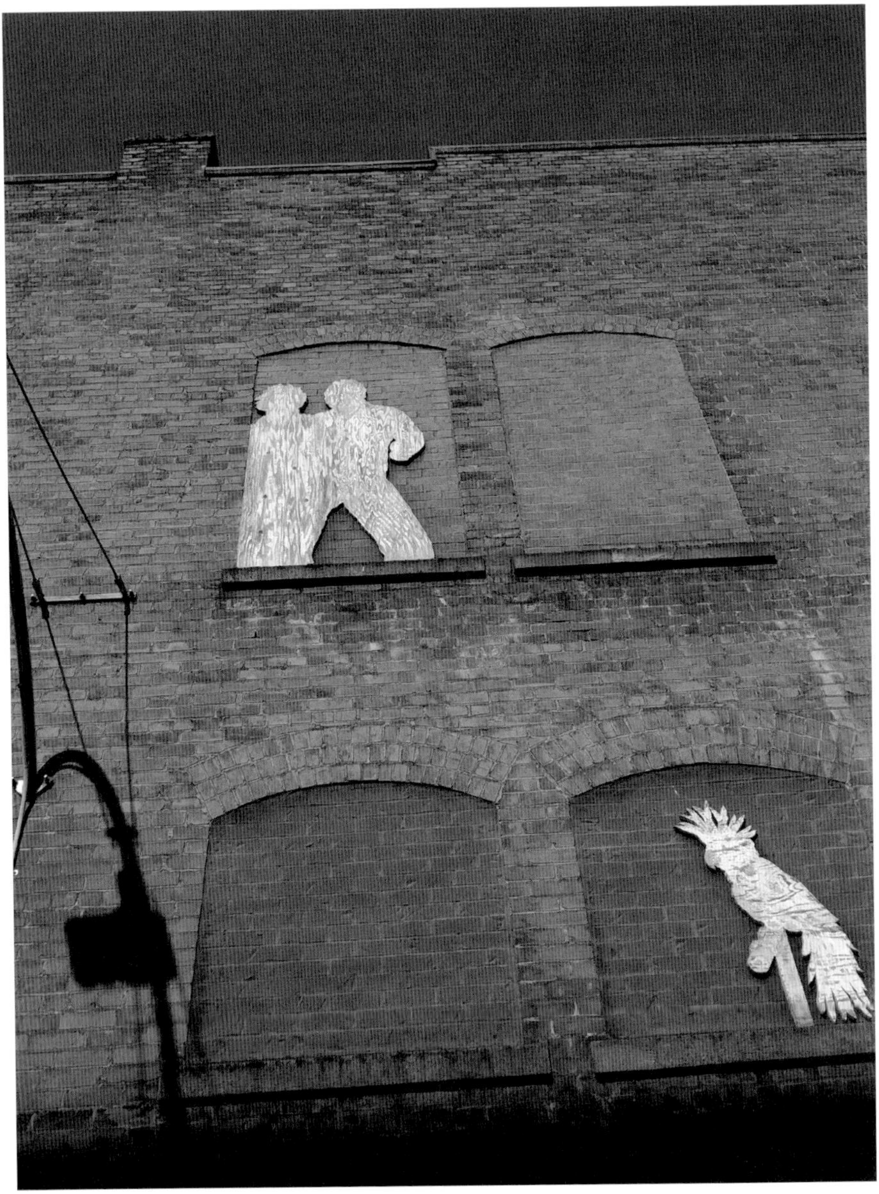

Alley wall with human figures. *Photo by Brittany Anne Dow.*

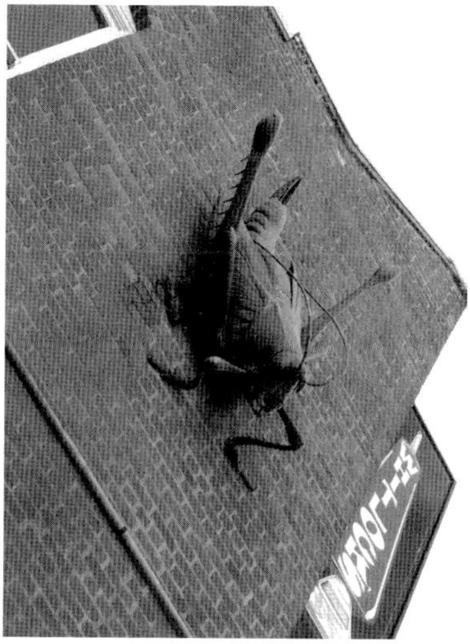

Salem's alleys contain artful and creative expressions. *Photo by Brittany Anne Dow.*

than one hundred years ago. A home close to that one has one of the most intolerable types of hauntings. A baby can often be heard crying frantically at night, even though an infant has not resided in the house for a very long time.

Another house, not far away, is said to be afflicted by the ghosts of an interracial couple who were murdered in the home's basement during an arson fire in the early 1980s.

Also close by, the historic Bush House on Mission and Twelfth Streets is said to be haunted. In the early 1900s, a girl with schizophrenia is said to have called the massive Bush House home. Well, her part of the home, as it turns out, was the basement, where she was kept hidden away from the world. The girl, according to reports, was shunned and lived a cold, lonely life. Her ghost, it is said, frequently turns the thermostat up, in an apparent attempt to warm the cold structure where she lived the extent of her sad life.

Once, an employee at Bush House was fully convinced that a ghost was making noises on the second floor. Further inspection revealed that a tree brushing against the house in the wind was the culprit. One can never be entirely sure.

OFFICER DOWN

An unexpected series of events surround the only shooting death of a Salem, Oregon police officer. This officer's last watch ended on October 1, 1909. He was killed in the line of duty.[31]

While people who murder police officers today are viewed with great contempt and almost always are placed in prison for life, the man who killed Officer Thomas M. Eckhart—a forty-five-year-old father of five children—got a slap on the wrist and lived to murder again.[32]

As the *Statesman Journal*'s Capi Lynn wrote in her article "Fallen Salem Police Officer Part of History," the *Daily Oregon Statesman* reported that Eckhart's funeral "was one of the most largely attended of any ever held in the city, people from every walk of life meeting to pay a last tribute to his memory."

The Salem Heritage Network Blogspot has a number of details about the crime.[33] Thomas M. Eckhart arrested a man named George Meyers for horse theft. As he was being led to jail, Meyers brandished a .38 caliber pistol and shot Officer Eckhart. Meyers was persuaded to turn himself in, which he did. His first trial was declared a mistrial.

Eckhart had been a police officer for ten months. Sadly, no pictures of Eckhart, who had also served as the Salem fire chief, are known to exist. Yet the family has maintained as much history on his life and death as possible. He was never forgotten. Recent additional information from Brian Goforth, Thomas Eckhart's great-grandson, is posted on the Heritage Blog:

> *Following the second trial, Meyers was sentenced to the Oregon State Prison. He was sentenced in 1911 (that's how long it took for the two trials to play out) and served about two years. According to the newspaper articles, he apparently was a model prisoner and was given privileges such as work releases. He was pardoned by the then-governor Oregon governor Oswald West in 1913. The newspaper reported that Meyers went to Seattle and lived there for a time. In 1915, again as reported in the newspaper, Meyers stopped in Salem to visit family and friends on his way to San Francisco. He told people that he was going to San Francisco to get married. According to the newspaper, when he arrived in San Francisco, he found that the woman he was to marry had married someone else. He shot and killed her, then took his own life! How's that for a twist of events?*

How and why the public did not demand that this man be incarcerated for life or hanged is not known. The story could not stand in greater contrast to the practices observed for fallen officers today.

This was the obituary for Thomas Eckhart as published by the *Daily Oregon Statesman* on October 2, 1909:

> *The life of one of Salem's brave police officers was ended yesterday afternoon through his being the victim of a murderous attack in the early morning hours. The bullet which caused the demise of good Tom Eckhart was fired from a pistol in the hands of a young resident of this city whose*

> *career has not been of the best sort for some month, and who, although at large at the time of this writing, will surely be apprehended and punished. But the punishment of the desperate young man, no matter how severe the penalty, will not bring back Tom Eckhart, good citizen, faithful officer, esteemed by everybody who knew him. It is a sad case, in all its bearings.*

Thomas Eckhart is buried in Pioneer Cemetery beside his wife, Rose. His name is also inscribed at the National Law Enforcement Memorial in Washington, D.C.

Graveyard Ghosts

Salem and the surrounding areas host a number of old cemeteries. Perhaps the most famous is the haunted Pioneer Cemetery on South Commercial Street. Another is the Jason Lee Cemetery on D Street, which is the resting place of its namesake as well as a number of other Salem pioneers.

Long believed to be haunted, there are many reports of things in the Pioneer Cemetery that are not of this earth, at least in the traditional sense. In the old cemetery, an angry ghost is said to watch you from a tree. Many people have reported experiencing an unwelcome feeling while visiting.

Other sounds can be heard in this otherwise quiet place, particularly in the summer, when the gates stay open longer. Sounds of babies and children crying are not uncommon. Mysterious sounds actually seem to originate from the graves themselves.

A Murderous Mom

Paranormal investigators believe the Pioneer Cemetery is haunted by a number of entities. One is described as a woman who, in the early 1900s, murdered her four children by administering poison before taking it herself. That particular family is buried in the northwest corner of the cemetery in unmarked graves.

The *Statesman Journal* reviewed the terrible story on June 4, 2015, in an article titled "Salem Tragedy in 1912: Mother Poisoned Four Children."[34] The woman's name was Lucy Jellison. She was thirty-nine at the time of her death. Her children ranged in age from three to fifteen. They were sons Harland (fifteen) and Raymond (three) and daughters Espey (twelve) and Maud (eight). Lucy dressed her children in freshly washed nightclothes on March 2, 1912, and gave them each potassium cyanide in a tent in their backyard at 469 North Liberty Street, the location today of Salem's downtown mall.

Due to her poverty, Jellison had moved out of the house, subleased it to other people and moved she and her children into the backyard.

Jellison actually sent a letter to the Salem Police chief detailing her reasons for taking the lives of her children. She blamed poverty. Her letter read as follows, "I know the law requires investigation." She also wrote, "Do as little as possible."

"The plain fact is I cannot earn enough alone to keep my family. Someone induced my boy to leave, and I am too ill to work. I cannot see them starve. There is a little money, $21, in my purse. Make it bury us all together." Their bodies were found the day after the murder. Jellison, who had been married three times, worked as a seamstress and dressmaker.

I know a number of people who have had odd and unusual experiences in these old historic cemeteries. With stories like this one, it is not surprising. Several groups of paranormal researchers have visited the old graveyards late at night and have come away with eerie recordings, both audio and video, of what almost certainly seems to be ghost-generated activity.

It is an experience when you are visiting either place to try to comprehend the sheer number of deaths and funerals they represent. From mid-nineteenth-century to modern-day graves, these are resting places where every soul does not seem to be entirely restful—indeed "restive" might be a better description.

17
Ghosts in Salem's Schools

The saddest stories are always the ones that involve young people dying before their time. The ghost of a high school actor is believed to be the source of strange events at the McNary High School theater.

An article by Capi Lynn, "A Favorite Haunt," published by the *Statesman Journal* on October 31, 2002, explains the bizarre and mysterious events that happen in the theater.[35] Creaking sounds are heard coming from above the stage, and lights go on and off—standard fare for poltergeists. Items from the stage go missing and then show up later, often disappearing again.

Lynn explains that members of the drama department believe it is the ghost of a former student. Sean Sadowski, a former drama student, was killed in a tragic car accident on June 17, 1986. He was riding in the back of a pickup truck that went over an embankment near Dallas. Sean suffered severe head injuries and died as a result.

Those who talk about the disturbances do not view the matter with fear. They say Sean was an enthusiastic student who loved acting.

Staff and students over the years have had varying degrees of contact with Sean. Those drama students who have experienced the most frequent visitations from Sean are the serious actors who invest a great deal of time in their craft, like Sean did.

In a way, Sean went on living. His parents donated his organs, allowing multiple people to continue living. His heart went to a father of eight in Vancouver, Washington.

Sean is said to be mischievous as a ghost, but he never brings his antics during shows. He waits until he is in the company of the drama department members before cutting loose. A Hollywood-style star on the McNary campus honors Sean today. His life is remembered and would be even if there was no related ghost story. Sean had performed in a school presentation of *Grease* and was well liked—and still is.

Oregon School for the Deaf

The Oregon School for the Deaf has been serving students for many years in Salem. A boarding facility, the school has "The Nightmare Factory," one of the most spectacular Halloween haunted house displays in the nation.

But don't let the Halloween show get in the way. People have reported numerous sightings of ghosts and a particular shadow figure over the years, and many believe it is haunted.

A boys' dormitory is said to be one of the haunted sites. Three boys who were students were reportedly killed in a mysterious way. While this is widely reported, I have not been able to locate any information about it that would verify the three deaths, so it is unlikely that they actually happened.

A black figure, often referred to as a shadow person, has been seen by many students roaming the campus at night. Ghosts are said to have been seen in the girls' and boys' dorms.

Crystal Power + Light

Jim and Lisa Lind, owners of the jewelry and bead store Crystal Power & Light, moved into their commercial store in downtown Salem more than three decades ago. From the day they arrived, they knew they weren't alone. "My front door will open and close up to eight times a day," Jim Lind explains, adding, "It sure has freaked some people out!" His 1869 store was originally a harness and saddle shop.

He explains that there is a section in the floor of his store that lifts up and allows a person to access the area underneath his store. In that area, the Linds have located some unusual items, including Chinese medicine

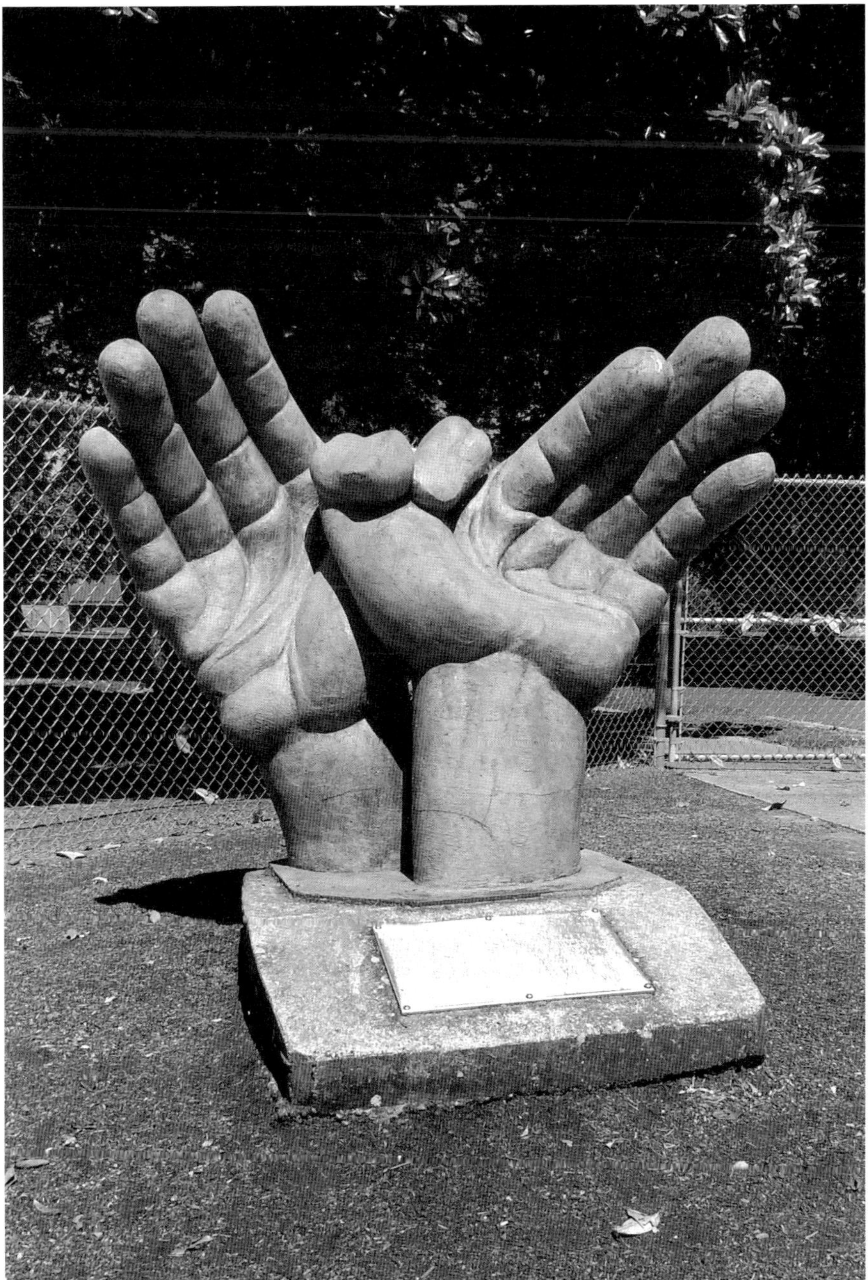

The Oregon School for the Deaf. *Photo by Brittany Anne Dow.*

bottles from the 1800s. Beneath the store are rows of trenches that resemble a World War I battlefield.

Jim Lind says other strange things have happened over the years at Crystal Power & Light. "One morning I came into work and the glass front of one of my display cabinets had exploded into thousands of pieces. I immediately assumed that someone had broken into the store, but there was no sign of forced entry, and nothing was missing." To this day, Jim remains stumped over what possibly could have caused the front of the display case to break into so many pieces. He says all of the glass landed on the floor, and no pieces were found inside of the display case, demonstrating that the glass absolutely broke from the inside.

Strange activities persist at Crystal Power & Light.

SALEM'S TALLEST BUILDING

In the late 1920s, a Salem man by the name of Thomas Livesly was inspired by a building he visited in New York City. In fact, he was so taken with the structure that he came to Salem and built his own version of the building.

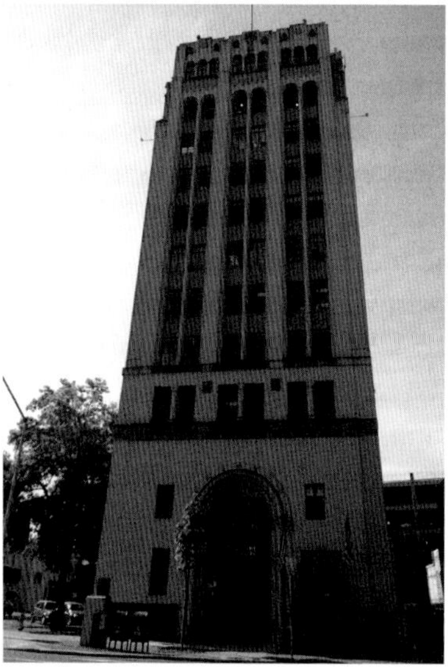

The tallest building in Salem, the Capital Center, by Brittany Anne Dow. *Courtesy of Brittany Anne Dow.*

To this day, Livesly's building, today known as the Capital Center, towers over Salem as the city's tallest structure.

Former employees describe a floating ball of white light that will follow a person on the building's second floor. The light is said to emit a disconcerting energy that makes a person want to flee.

The Capital Center was the scene of a tragic suicide in the 1970s that was witnessed by many in Oregon's capital city. Perhaps that event adds to the pool of ghosts that call the building home. In fact, each floor of this building has its own stories about things people witness yet can't explain.

18
Human Trafficking

Whether you are talking about 120 years ago or today, Oregon has seen some of the worst human trafficking in U.S. history. Starting with the Shanghai Tunnels in the late 1800s, where men were captured and forced into roles as mariner slaves and women were forced into sex trafficking, the problem has never gone away.

Salem is no stranger to the idea of human trafficking, though on a lesser scale. It was not that many years ago that Salem was the center of sex-slave trafficking, and it happened in the city's busy downtown. One of the girls held in bondage in what is now Café Shine was the daughter of a ranking Portland police commander. Café Shine is located at the former Six Ultralounge nightclub. Today, the facility is a house of prayer.

The facility's website acknowledges the crimes against humanity that took place here. "Years later when we were cleaning out the building and preparing to move in, evidence surfaced that human trafficking had taken place in this very building. Today, Café Shine is a testimony of God's faithfulness to redeem a space which was once a gateway of darkness into the city and use it for the purposes of His kingdom."

As the *Statesman Journal* explains in a February 22, 2014 article, Café Shine, located at 248 Liberty Street Northeast, exists at a downtown address with a checkered past.[36] "The previous tenant was the nightclub Six Ultralounge, which closed in late 2009 after the OLCC yanked its liquor license for a 'history of serious and persistent problems involving disturbances, lewd or unlawful activities.'"

The sex trafficking apparently went away without the help of local police. While it is referenced in many articles and even in a new proposed movie, there are many descriptions of what the new owners found when they took control of the historic property.

Upstairs was a room painted bright red that was apparently used for prostitution. There is an "upskirt" viewing window where people would gather to peak at female customers who wore dresses or skirts. This all went on without anyone taking notice. The two previous clients of the buildings were also nightclubs; neither had a stellar reputation. Human trafficking, and sex trafficking in particular, continue to plague Oregon.

19

GHOSTS OF FIRE

Smoke was spotted coming from an elevator shaft at the Oregon State Capitol on April 25, 1935. Before firefighters arrived, the flames had reached the dome of the building.

The devastating fire started at 6:30 p.m., and firefighters from as far away as Portland responded to the blaze, aiding local fire agencies. In fact, firefighters showed up from all over western Oregon, using every technique to bring the fire under control. But it was all to no avail.

Sadly, one young man named Floyd McMullen would give his life to the effort. He was fighting the blaze with other Willamette University students in an effort to protect their campus buildings when a cornice from the northwest corner of the state capitol crashed down on the young student, who suffered a fractured skull and a crushed pelvis.

A sophomore at Willamette, McMullen had paid his way through college by working as a firefighter at the East Salem Fire Station. He survived his injuries initially but later died after being transported to the hospital.

Fire has ravaged Salem buildings and claimed many lives over the years. Of course, the state capitol itself has burned twice, in 1855 and again in 1935. A number of Chinese businesses burned in Salem in the late 1800s; those fires consumed numerous laundry facilities.

One corner, today a vacant lot, was a McMahon's Furniture store before the building was consumed by fire a few years ago. Every building that has ever been erected on that particular corner has gone up in flames. The first was a Chinese laundry facility. That building was ravaged by fire, taking a number of lives in the process. The Chinese who died in the fire are said to inhabit the area as ghosts.

Another deadly fire involving a Chinese laundry business occurred in 1885 at the intersection of Chemeketa and State Streets. Today, at the same location where a more modern building exists, a flight of stairs, long closed off, goes down to the underground.

20

Haunted Restaurants, Buildings and Stores

Salem has a large number of ghost stories that are associated with businesses. It is important to remember that in downtown Salem, nearly every building that isn't old exists in a location that has been occupied by one or more previous buildings.

There are so many curiosities in Salem! At the corner of Liberty and State Streets is the 1916 McGilchrist Building. It is situated in the block that once comprised Chinatown. It was under this building that an abandoned disco was found a few years ago after having been locked up and forgotten for decades.

In recent years, the McGilchrist Building has undergone an extensive $7 million restoration, but one thing about that building did not change: the front still displays inverted crosses from its original construction. They are unmistakable and extremely rare. For many people, the instinctive thought is that the inverted cross is an anti-Christian symbol. That certainly is true for many of the supposedly devil-worshiping heavy metal bands from the United States and Europe. But these inverted crosses are something entirely different.

The unusual design is called the Cross of Saint Peter or, more simply, Saint Peter's Cross. It is a symbol of Christian humility and is in no way anti-Christian in nature. The inverted cross draws mostly from Catholic tradition. It first came to light in the "Martyrdom of Peter," which may have predated the apocryphal Acts of Peter.

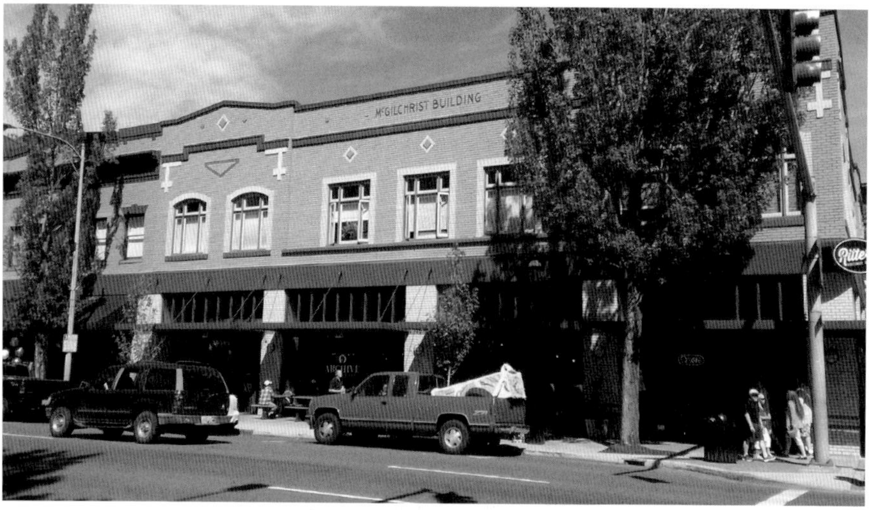

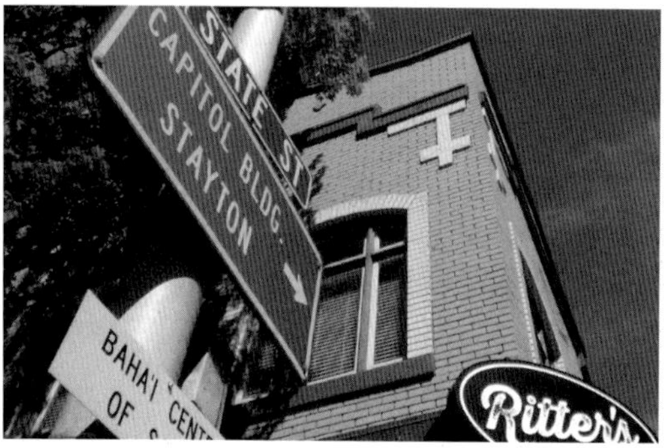

Above: McGilchrist Building in Salem. *Photo by Tim King.*

Left: Inverted cross at McGilchrist Building in Salem. *Photo by Tim King.*

The symbol dates to at least AD 200 and could have appeared sooner. Saint Peter, it was said, did not want to be crucified in the same manner as Jesus, hence the inverted cross. There is no direct statement about Peter's cross being inverted, but the implication is clear. In some cases, Catholics see the inverted cross as a symbol of humility and unworthiness in relation to Jesus.

The group Catholic Answers states: "As a result of the manner in which he was crucified, the Church has used the upside down cross [without a corpus, so not a crucifix] to designate Peter, not Christ. The Pope, being the successor of Peter, employs the symbol of the upside down cross as a symbolic reminder of St. Peter's humility and heroic martyrdom. Unlike an upside down crucifix, which seeks to invert and subvert it's meaning, there is nothing satanic about an upside down cross."[37]

BIKE SHOP GHOST

The Bike Peddler at 174 Commercial Street Northeast in Salem has been doing business since 1974 in the same location. This store has thrived for a long time, and among the living employees is the ghost of a man who walks back and forth in the underground area, continually entering the old photo shop that existed in the same space many years ago.

"It's creepy," said the son of Jim, the shop's manager. From what they describe, they could have a residual ghost on their property, or perhaps an intelligent ghost. It isn't always easy to know.

As noted earlier in this book, when the transparent image of a human being is seen repeating the same action over and over again, as this apparition does, it often falls into the category of residual spirit. But it has nonetheless been startling for the employees of the Bike Peddler.

One thing is certain, they are somewhat adjusted to this image of a man dressed in old-time clothing who almost certainly was one of the main operators. The entity is obviously dedicated to its profession.

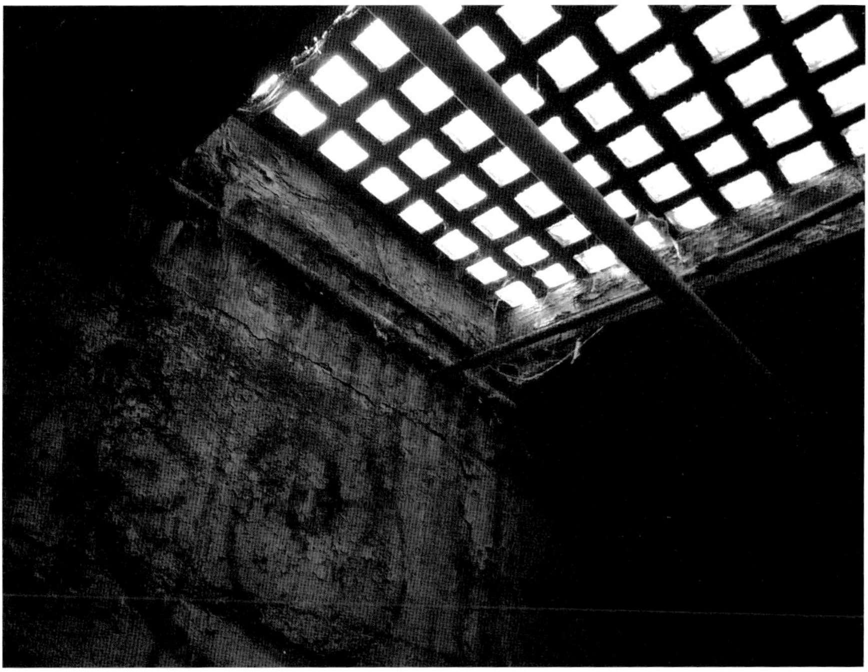

Photo taken in the area where a ghost is frequently sighted, beneath the Bike Peddler on Commercial Street in Salem. *Photo by Austin King.*

Ghost of a Little Girl in a Shoe Store

Another story that a number of people attest to involves the ghost of a little girl in the Footlocker shoe store located in Salem Center. For a number of years, the present site of the store happens to be situated over a former parking lot, where a little girl was struck by a car and killed many years ago.

Employees at the shoe store have reported seeing the little girl's ghost on numerous occasions. She is usually seen in the shoe room, where all of the shoes not on the retail shelves are kept.

The people who work for the store have to go to the shoe room frequently to see if the size a particular customer needs is in stock. This increases the frequency of visits to the room where the little girl is said to be.

One former employee who was very traumatized by the ghost told me that the girl was completely sad and lost.

Apparition at Hometown Buffet

One haunted restaurant story that often pops up on searches is the Hometown Buffet, at 636 Lancaster Drive. One person on the Shadowlands webpage writes about a bizarre experience in the buffet on an evening out for a family dinner.[38] In the bathroom, this person witnessed what they describe as a woman in a white 1950s dress, running past them and entering the last stall. The woman is described as having pure white skin and hair that matched her dress, void of all color, appearing very ghostly.

Many strange stories have originated from within this building, including of objects being moved by unseen hands, doors being opened and slammed closed and voices that are heard but not traceable to any particular source.

Another Haunted Restaurant

In truth, several more restaurants in Salem are believed to be haunted, including Shari's Restaurant on South Commercial in Salem.

Items float away from the kitchen, a ghostly apparition has been spotted by numerous employees, and loud sounds of people yelling and fighting come from a particular area in the back of the restaurant. Employees have never discovered a source.

Considering that human beings have inhabited what we now call Salem, Oregon, for thousands of years, it is hard to know or even imagine the source of so many reported hauntings.

Ghosts in the Pantry

There are two Plaid Pantry convenience stores in Salem, one on Mission Street and one on River Road, that employees swear are haunted. I have heard many of the stories firsthand, and some are truly chilling. They have aspects of a scientific factor, where something is definitely taking place in a way that in some cases can be documented, explainable or not.

The River Road store is known for having its door opened by phantom hands. Then, with no customer entering the store, the trip sensor goes off and beeps, indicating that someone has walked inside. This is frequently observed during the graveyard shift. The store is very close to haunted Minto Brown Park.

The Mission Street store, I am told, has the same thing happen. The sensor will go off when nobody is in the store. This is very chilling for workers on the graveyard shift, who have to observe a number of precautions for safety and security.

Employees at the Mission Street store have told me they also hear bottles rattling and being moved in the cooler when they are alone. In those cases, the sensors that determine if a person is in the room…remain silent.

Imagine the humanity that flows through these establishments. Many customers are homeless, broken people who seem to buy food only at intervals when their Oregon Trail Cards, the equivalent of food stamps, are refunded each month.

Another Plaid Pantry store, on State Street in Salem, is the closest retail establishment to the historic Oregon State Penitentiary. Inevitably, long-term inmates are released after serving their time, and many are very old upon their release.

I have heard stories about these men, wearing 1970s or '80s clothing, walking into the store and looking around with total amazement. The lifetimes of some of these just-released prisoners perhaps overlapped with computers, but many have been incarcerated for so long that they have absolutely no idea what they are seeing.

One story, about a man with long gray hair wearing clothing that was clearly from the 1970s, was completely riveting. He had never heard of a debit card, had no idea what an ATM was, had never seen a computerized cash register and was totally amazed and taken aback by the changes that had taken place in the world during his decades behind bars.

When this man was imprisoned, candy bars were $0.25, cigarettes were less than $1.00. He remembers what a big deal it was when a six-pack of his favorite beer went from $1.29 to $1.49.

The man was a little disturbed and far out of his element. He ended up leaving without buying anything, though he had longed for a beer for more than forty years. He must have been disappointed when he entered the next store and found the prices the same.

I believe I saw that same man, based on his description, the same day in downtown Salem, near the Mission.

SALEM'S LIVING GHOSTS

Salem's housing-challenged community is, and has been from the beginning, a cultural melting pot.

Newly released jail and prison inmates are an aspect of the thousands of homeless people living out of sight and out of mind in Salem, Oregon.

Many of these unfortunate souls are mentally ill but untreated. A percentage of these folks were housed at the Fairview Training Center, which began closing down in the 1980s during the presidency of Ronald Reagan. They will often talk about Fairview and the things they witnessed and survived there.

Within the *houseless* community, most of whom live in camps outside of the city, are a growing number of U.S. military veterans. Among them are combat vets from the Vietnam, Afghanistan and Iraq Wars. They, like many civilians in the houseless community, suffer from post-traumatic stress disorder (PTSD), which makes life extremely challenging.

The military veterans also take leadership roles and maintain a degree of safety and security that city officials are oblivious to. I point that out because Salem routinely "purges" the homeless from the camps where they attempt to have an existence, sending these people—many of whom are mentally unstable—fleeing onto the city's streets, mostly downtown, where too many wander dazed and confused, wondering where that next tent, sleeping bag and other necessities for living homeless almost off the land will come from.

They live among a population largely comprising state and government employees. They coexist with the city's indigent population when they are downtown.

What I have learned over the years is that the homeless community is greatly ignored and abused in Oregon. This is a community particularly sensitive to things that are paranormal or supernatural. Some are plagued with afflictions that cause great stress and create an inability to cope.

Much more can be done, and has to be done, to change the difficult situation that keeps people homeless, untreated and unable to live a decent life.

In its own way, the story of the homeless is similar to the abuse of mental patients in Oregon's earlier years. Oregon officials are often slow to comprehend the ramifications of their largely unkind and immoral political decisions.

People who exist in Salem's homeless community talk about things that are alarming, things that happen in the night that no person would want to experience. The homeless are unsheltered and unprotected from nocturnal spirits. While one must bear in mind that a percentage of the homeless population has mental issues, it is also interesting to consider what people who are mentally ill might be able to see and decipher from the "other side."

PERCEPTIONS

I have to admit that I've given a lot of thought to this subject over the years. What is it about people claiming they hear voices in their heads that disturbs me so much?

I think I know.

Many people hear voices in their heads. Perhaps their inner psyches are not creating these illusions.

The Exorcist introduced people to a totally different take on religion and spirituality in the 1970s, one touching on demonic possession.[39] As referenced earlier in this book, many paranormal investigators believe that there are demonic possessions of ghosts. If this is true, it would explain why some haunted places or situations are more intense than others.

Some ghosts exhibit no signs of negativity. More than once, however, clairvoyants I have worked with tell me that the ghosts they can see do not like being stared at by a human being with clear sight.

The clairvoyants, or mediums, have told me that great hostility emanates from these spirits when they realize they are visible to a living person with psychic power.

21
The Sky Is the Limit

No book on paranormal activity would be complete without a section on UFOs. It is particularly true for this book, because so many reports have been made in both Salem and Keizer, the city to Salem's immediate north.

When I was a small boy growing up in Los Angeles, around the age of eight, neighbor kids and I saw something very strange in the sky. It was broad daylight, but several multicolored objects traveled through the sky like nothing I had ever seen. I called my mom, who ultimately decided to call the local newspaper. To my surprise, my name was in an article along with a cartoon with little spaceships. The newspaper, the *Huntington Park Daily Signal*, talked to the air force about the sighting and was told it was "weather balloons," which is totally unsurprising.

But the event left a picture in my mind, and it is not the only time I have witnessed similar things. One day in Las Vegas when I worked for the city's NBC station, KVBC (KSNV today), I was standing on the sidewalk by our back doors having a cigarette with the weather anchor. We both looked up and saw silvery objects ascending into the sky at a very high rate of speed. We never learned any more about it, but it left a chilling vision.

Back to Salem, an incredible sighting was made on September 27, 2016, just east of the city, according to the report of a man who saw what he described as twenty to thirty bright objects. According to a report at ufosnw.com, the man thought some of the objects were having a hard time getting airborne.[40] He suspected they were helicopters, but they made no sound.

Amazingly, the man said the flying objects looked like "floating houses," and he described seeing windows. He reported seeing a blue pulse of light coming from the flying objects and says he could not start his car after this encounter, eventually requiring a jump-start to get his engine going.

One witness referenced on the website says it was October 1999, in a rural part of Keizer, Oregon, where they witnessed a large, silent triangle craft glide above and over them. The witness said the craft had a large orange circle in the center and three white lights on each of the craft's three points.

On October 20, 2016, a Salem woman traveling with her son and husband reported seeing three orange lights that moved north in the night sky. The woman, who lives on a rural property, was tending her horses when she first saw the lights, mistaking them for stars. However, the movement of the lights caused her to realize she was not seeing something normal or necessarily of this world. She said the lights would stop, hover in place and then begin to move again. She said that her husband and son saw the same thing. She said there were bright flashes of blue and red light and that the craft remained visible for five minutes.

A sighting from March 19, 2016, would have to have been seen by many people, according to a witness who reported seeing the UFO while driving toward Salem from Albany. The person reported that everyone in their vehicle saw a white light ahead of them on the left side of the highway. The primary witness said it was thought to be a streetlight for a moment, but then the sudden realization that it was something else confronted them. "I rolled my window down and saw a triangular UFO type object with three white lights on each side. It looked like it was rotating and was so close I could see the intricate details on the aircraft."

After the witnesses passed the craft, it began slowly hovering behind their vehicle, following them. The witness told ufosnw.com, "I didn't want to look again because I was creeped out, but it finally disappeared."

These sightings happen constantly in the Salem area and throughout Oregon. Many are photographed; video is used to record different sightings, and there are other elements of credibility.

22

SALEM'S CRUELEST KILLER

Jerome Henry "Jerry" Brudos, who was born on January 31, 1939, and died behind bars at the age of sixty-seven on March 28, 2006, represents one of the saddest stories in the history of Salem.

Born of more than adequate intelligence, Brudos was a talented radio engineer, yet he would go down in history as one of the sickest criminals that Salem would ever know. It was a case of abuse leading to more sick abuse.

In his case, having a high IQ was not enough. Bearing in mind the flagrant abuse of his mother, who never really wanted another male child, it seems like the demons in Brudos's head never met resistance. Dubbed the "Lust Killer," and also the "Shoe Fetish Killer," Brudos had an unhappy childhood.[41]

SHOE FETISH DEVELOPED EARLY

Made to feel second best, he was an average-looking kid, though he was never described as handsome. When he was a small boy, Brudos found a pair of women's high-heeled shoes in a dumpster. His mother taunted Brudos with those shoes; by some accounts, he was forced to wear them while his mother humiliated him.

One thing is certain, those shoes and the bizarre actions of his mother led to his foot and shoe fetish. Later, in the act of kidnapping, raping and torturing his victims, Brudos would sometimes remove a foot from the girls and place it in his freezer.

Brudos also developed an intense interest in stockings and girls' underwear. As a teenager, he would attack girls and knock them down in order to steal their shoes. He amassed quite a collection, police would later learn. After being caught and sent to prison, Brudos maintained catalogues of women's undergarments for his personal pleasure and amusement. That was not illegal in the prison, under the auspices of the Oregon Department of Corrections.

Over the years, I have talked to numerous people who knew Brudos inside the penitentiary, either fellow inmates or former correctional officers. They all talked about how talented he was at repairing computers, and apparently he maintained computers for a number of prison officials. Men who knew Brudos describe him as an amiable person, easy to get along with.

Going back to the teenage years, Brudos was so aggressive and violent toward females that he would find himself incarcerated at the Oregon State Hospital at the age of seventeen.

Among other crimes, he invited a neighbor girl over one day, and then, after she was inside his house, he excused himself. A few moments later, a male of the same height and weight (it was Brudos) wearing a mask attacked the girl and forced her to remove her clothing. He then photographed her nude body. Fleeing from the room, Brudos returned a few moments later and told the girl that a man had knocked him out and that he had just regained consciousness. The girl didn't buy it. She fled the residence.

Shortly after that, Brudos was placed in the state mental hospital. Here, in the company of doctors and medical staff, Brudos shared in detail his plans of having elaborate torture chambers where he would bring his future victims and, without adding detail, do terrible things to them. So, knowing that they had a deranged, violent sex criminal in their midst who had plans of bringing severe harm to women and girls, the state hospital did the last thing anyone would imagine: it simply released him. Go figure.

Brudos served a short stint in the U.S. Army, stationed in Monterey, California. After being discharged, he returned to Oregon. Shortly after that, his crime spree began.

In 1968, women began to disappear from the city of Portland. He took one girl from Salem, but Brudos also cruised in search of his victims. His last noted activity before he was taken into custody was around the Oregon State University (OSU) campus in Corvallis.

Linda Slawson, nineteen, made the fatal mistake of knocking on Jerry Brudos's door. She would be the first of his victims to have her foot cut off and placed in his refrigerator. Ann Rule wrote about Brudos's crimes in great detail in her book *Lust Killer*.

Brudos had a family, and he made them keep their distance from his private garage/shed in his backyard. His wife was never allowed to enter the outbuilding, which is where he kept, abused and murdered the girls.

His next victim, Jan Whitney, was twenty-three. She fell prey to Brudos when her car broke down while driving home from college in November 1968. This poor girl didn't even make it out of her own car. Brudos admitted strangling her and taking her body back to his workshop, where he continued to violate her dead body over the next several days while she hung from a hook in the ceiling.

The third victim was nineteen-year-old Karen Sprinkler. She was taken from a parking garage located above a department store, where she was supposed to meet her mother for lunch. Brudos forced her into his car at gunpoint. After taking her back to his outbuilding, he raped her and forced her to pose for photographs wearing various articles of women's underwear that Brudos had collected. Brudos would later admit that, like the previous victim, he continued to violate her corpse for several days after killing her.

Brudos's last victim was a twenty-two-year-old named Linda Salee. I recently spoke to a woman who grew up with Salee. She spoke of the enormous sadness that her murder brought. Fortunately, Salee would be Brudos's last victim. He disposed of the girl's remains by dumping them in a lake near what is now Salem City Hall. He disposed of other remains in Long Tom River.

Brudos had no limits. After killing the four girls, he began prowling the campus of OSU, talking to girls and claiming to be a Vietnam veteran, raising significant concerns about the war. When the police finally caught his trail, a pair of detectives visited the Brudos house to see what they could glean. A bonus of unimaginable proportions greeted them.

As Brudos confidently visited with the detectives at his front door, he noticed that one kept looking at a coil of rope on a shelf by his front door. Brudos took note and asked the detective if he would like a piece of the rope. Incredibly, this was the same rope that Brudos had used to tie his victims. It was a dead match for the rope used on the girls whose remains were located in the Salem lake and the Long Tom River.

Brudos thought he was intellectually superior to the police. He could not have been more wrong.

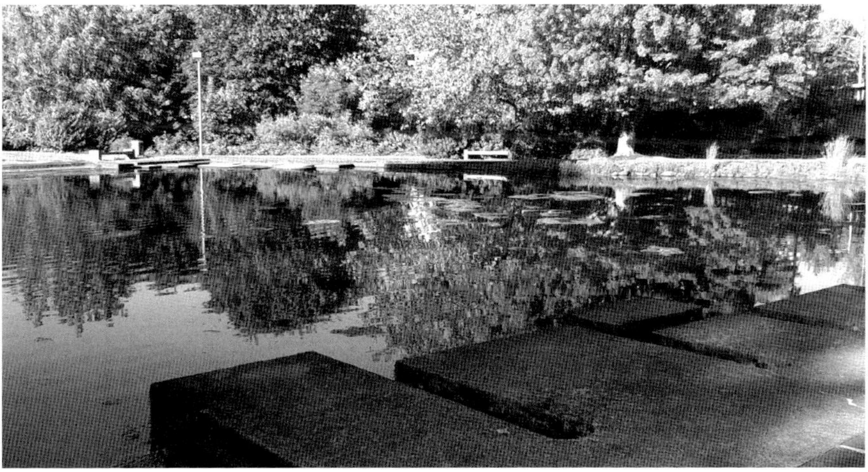

Area adjacent to Salem City Hall where serial killer Jerry Brudos dumped remains of his female victims. *Photo by Tim King.*

I interviewed a retired Salem detective named Jim Strovink in 2003 about his memories of the Brudos case. He explained to me that he visited Brudos shortly after he was incarcerated in the Oregon State Penitentiary. He hoped to glean clues from Brudos about other possibly missing girls. In truth, Brudos was a braggart, and he seemed to enjoy talking about his crimes. In all likelihood, the four young women were his only victims.

Strovink said he looked Brudos in the eye and asked him if he ever felt bad for the crimes he had committed. He asked him if he ever considered how the girls must be missed, particularly on holidays. Brudos, the retired detective said, simply picked up a piece of paper, wrinkled it into a ball and dropped it on the floor, stating in a matter-of-fact way, "It bothers me that much."

Brudos was an unusual killer in that he was intelligent, though not nearly as much as he believed. He was also void of emotion or guilt over his heinous crimes.

Sadly, the house Brudos lived in, the very home where he committed his crimes, still stands, as does his garage workshop.

Prior to his arrest, a vehicle crashed into the garage of the Brudos house while one girl was inside of the building. Though there was a full emergency response, the police did not observe or learn that the unfortunate girl was just a few feet away. It is hard to second-guess events like that; one can only imagine that the police simply didn't have a vantage point or any reason for suspicion, as the home was simply the scene of a random traffic accident.

How could that garage possibly not be haunted? Can you imagine?

Final Thoughts

I hope this book leaves you with more knowledge so you can investigate these crimes, tragedies and mysteries yourself.

Salem, Oregon, is unique in that it has far more than the average number of ghost stories. Just remember that, to the best of our understanding, ghosts are what remains on earth from a living person.

All human beings deserve respect; it is an essential component, and therefore the dead deserve as much or more respect. We all will eventually die; we are naturally curious about what that means and what process we go through after leaving this earth.

Moreover, throughout our lifetimes we will inevitably encounter a ghost or spirit that we do not understand. The more you know about this, the better, in my humble opinion.

That is why I chose to write *Haunted Salem, Oregon*. I sincerely hope you enjoyed it!

Notes

Preface

1. *Oregonian*, 1991, article about Knight Hall.
2. "A Cold Journey through the Afghanistan High Country to a Castle for Christmas," Salem-News.com, December 26, 2006, http://www.salem-news.com/articles/december262006/tim_122606.php.

Chapter 1

3. "Chinese Americans," Salem History, http://www.salemhistory.net/people/chinese_americans.htm.
4. "Two Historians Explore Salem's Underground System Piece by Piece," KPTV FOX 12, February 15, 2017, http://www.kptv.com/story/34516530/two-historians-explore-salems-underground-system-piece-by-piece.
5. Benjamin Franklin Biser, *Elements of Glass and Glass Making* (Julius Arnold Koch, 1899).

Chapter 3

6. "Haunted Salem," Salem Online History, www.salemhistory.net/brief_history/haunted_salem.htm.

7. Diane L. Goeres-Gardner, *Necktie Parties: A History of Legal Executions in Oregon, 1851–1905* (Caldwell, ID: Caxton, 2005).
8. Timothy C. McFetridge, *Rachel's Son, Jackson* (New York: Page Publishing, 2016).
9. Sarah Hunt Steeves, *Book of Remembrance of Marion County Pioneers, 1840–1860* (Portland, OR: Berncliff Press, 1927).
10. Ibid., 12–15.

Chapter 4

11. "Oregon's Forgotten Hospital," *Oregonian*, January 9, 2005, http://www.oregonlive.com/editors/index.ssf/2013/04/oregons_forgotten_hospital.html.
12. Nigel Jaquiss, "Federal Public Defender Files Motion to Free Frank Gable in Michael Francke Murder," *Willamette Week Portland*, October 17, 2014, www.wweek.com/portland/blog-32339-federal-public-defender-files-motion-to-free-frank-gable-in-michael-francke-murder.html.
13. Ken Kesey, *One Flew Over the Cuckoo's Nest* (New York: Penguin, 1962).

Chapter 5

14. Stephen Wagner, "Edison and the Ghost Machine," ThoughtCo.com, May 4, 2017, https://www.thoughtco.com/edison-and-the-ghost-machine-2594017.

Chapter 6

15. Capi Lynn, "Mystery Cloaks 1895 Murder of Japanese Woman," *Salem Statesman Journal*, July 30, 2015, www.statesmanjournal.com/story/news/local/headstones-of-history/2015/07/30/mystery-cloaks-murder-japanese-woman-salem/30907989.

Chapter 7

16. "Mother and Daughter See 'Troll' Near House, Sleep in Motel that Night," OregonBigfoot.com, July 5, 2002, www.oregonbigfoot.com/report_detail.php?id=00325.
17. John Beeson, *A Plea for the Indians; with Facts and Features of the Late War in Oregon* (New York, 1857), 926.
18. "Observations of John Minto, Salem, Oregon 1874," NDN History Research, https://ndnhistoryresearch.wordpress.com/2015/05/29/participant-observations-of-john-minto-salem-oregon-1874.

Chapter 11

19. "Apology for Oregon Forced Sterilizations," Associated Press, December 3, 2002, www.articles.latimes.com/2002/dec/03/nation/na-sterile3.
20. *10 Days in a Madhouse*. Imdb.com, 2015, www.imdb.com/title/tt3453052.

Chapter 12

21. "Sherry Melissa Eyerly," the Charley Project, www.charleyproject.org/cases/e/eyerly_sherry.html.
22. "Minto Brown Park EVP Sherry Eyerly Shack Salem Oregon Ghost 'Megan'," YouTube, https://www.youtube.com/watch?v=wvOt6NDfXQI.
23. Andy Hall, "Destruction," Civil War Talk, https://civilwartalk.com/threads/steamers-era-and-not-nypl.121226.

Chapter 13

24. "Madam and Forty-Niner, Maggie Gardner Led Double Life in Salem and Out East," Capital Taps, May 15, 2010, capitaltaps.blogspot.com/2010/05/madam-and-forty-niner-maggie-gardner.html.

Chapter 14

25. Joseph "Bunko" Kelly, *Thirteen Years in the Oregon Penitentiary* (Whitefish, MT: Kessinger Publishing, 1908). https://www.amazon.com/Thirteen-Oregon-Penitentiary-Joseph-Kelley/dp/1166163016.

Chapter 15

26. J. Holcombe and D. Jacobson, "The Great 1918 Flu Pandemic Was Not Due to Flu…or a Virus," Salem-News.com, April 14, 2011, www.salem-news.com/articles/april142011/1918-flu.php.
27. Kayley Mendenhall, "Spanish Influenza in 1918 Killed 3,688 People in Oregon," *Bulletin* (Bend, OR), August 13, 2006, www.bendbulletin.com/news/1521670-151/spanish-influenza-in-1918-killed-3688-people-in.
28. Marc Dadigan, "Unmarked Graves Discovered at Chemawa Indian School," Al Jazeera, January 2, 2016, www.aljazeera.com/indepth/features/2016/01/unearthing-dark-native-boarding-school-160103072842972.html.
29. Randy Gordon, "McKinley Elementary School," Salem Online History, www.salemhistory.net/education/mckinley.htm.

Chapter 16

30. "Haunted Salem," Salem Online History, www.salemhistory.net/brief_history/haunted_salem.htm.
31. "Thomas M. Eckhart," Salem Pioneer Cemetery, www.salempioneercemetery.org/records/pf_display_record.php?id=2176.
32. Capi Lynn, "Fallen Salem Police Officer Part of History," *Statesman Journal*, October 1, 2009, 1.
33. "Salem in 1909," Salem Heritage Network, April 1, 2010, http://www.salem-heritage-network.blogspot.com/2010/04/salem-in-1909.html.
34. Capi Lynn, "Salem Tragedy in 1912: Mother Poisoned Four Children," *Statesman Journal*, June 4, 2015, www.wausaudailyherald.com/story/news/headstones-of-history/2015/06/04/salem-tragedy-mother-poisoned-four-children/28516001.

Chapter 17

35. Capi Lynn, "From the *Statesman Journal* Archives: A Salem Ghost Story," *Statesman Journal*, October 20, 2015, www.statesmanjournal.com/story/life/2015/10/20/from-the-archives-a-salem-ghost-story/74309600.

Chapter 18

36. "Redeeming Space," *Statesman Journal*, February 22, 2014, www.statesmanjournal.com/story/news/2014/02/23/redeeming-space/5747229.

Chapter 20

37. Hector Molina, "The Upside Down Cross: Satanic or Symbolic?" Catholic Answers, July 17, 2014, https://www.catholic.com/magazine/online-edition/the-upside-down-cross-satanic-or-symbolic.
38. "Haunted Places in Oregon," The Shadowlands. www.theshadowlands.net/places/oregon.htm.
39. *The Exorcist*. Imdb.com. www.imdb.com/title/tt0070047.

Chapter 21

40. "Several See Hovering White Object. Photos & Video Taken," ufosnw.com, August 9, 2016, www.ufosnw.com/newsite/several-see-hovering-white-object-photos-video-taken.

Chapter 22

41. Ann Rule and Andy Stack, *Lust Killer*. Updated edition (New York: Penguin, 1988).

About the Author

Tim King was born in Lynwood, California, in Los Angeles County, in 1963. His family was unique and offbeat, ahead of their time in many ways. Tim's dad built one of the first motorhomes in America, shortly after World War II.

Cars, motorcycles, surfing and the supernatural were Tim's personal passions—and still are.

After serving in the United States Marine Corps, Tim attended Cuesta College in San Luis Obispo and, by March 1988, attained his first media job as a news anchor at a small cable TV station on the Oregon coast, TV10. Tim's next role was as a radio news director, and he thrived at an AM/FM combo, KBCH/KCRF, in the early 1990s, earning his first award for broadcasting from the Associated Press.

His next project was to produce a television documentary about the sole survivor of a B-17 bomber crash on the Oregon Coast. *Fallen Fortress at Cape Lookout* aired twice on Oregon Public Broadcasting in 1993, earning excellent reviews. The story was told through the eyes and recollections of the plane's bombardier, who was the only aviator to survive the fiery crash that claimed nine lives.

In 1995, Tim was hired to work for the NBC station in Yuma, Arizona, KYMA, and spent the next two years covering stories from this hot, sometimes lonely but extremely interesting part of the country, located right next to the U.S. border with Mexico.

From there it was on to Las Vegas. Tim would spend the next five years there, working for the NBC station, KVBC News 3, and then at KVVU FOX 5. He covered many incredible stories here and was part of the first news team in the world to interview Evander Holyfield after Mike Tyson had bitten off part of his ear. Murders of every variety, all types of Strip-oriented crime and historical subjects, like the B-29 bomber that crashed in Lake Mead shortly after World War II, were stories Tim pursued.

He returned to Oregon in 2002, working initially in the Portland TV market as a freelance news photojournalist, then taking a position as an assignment editor with the Portland ABC affiliate, KATU. Shortly after being hired, Tim was reassigned as a photojournalist/reporter to the city of Salem, where he covered news for the station until 2006.

In 2004, he founded Salem-News.com, a news agency that is thriving almost fourteen years later. During his ten years as Salem-News.com's news editor, Tim built a team of more than 125 writers in almost thirty countries, specializing in political news with an emphasis on human-rights violations and war crimes.

Tim's next assignment was unlike all the rest. He made plans to travel to Afghanistan to cover the war through the eyes of Oregon National Guard soldiers deployed there during the winter of 2006–07. Based with the Oregon Guard's Forty-First Brigade Combat Team, Tim reported for KPTV Oregon FOX 12 and Salem-News.com for two months in the war zone, sending back thirty reports during that time. He covered operations in Kabul, Jalalabad, Ghazni and many other places in this historic country.

Then the saddest thing happened. Tim's parents, Charles and Nellie King, passed away on the same day in July 2007. This was a life-changing event. The next year, in the summer of 2008, Tim went to Iraq where he covered the war with the Oregon Guard, the U.S. Marines and the U.S. Army's 101st Airborne. He spent time in Ballad, Baghdad, al Anbar Province and other parts of Iraq.

In 2011, Tim was flown to Albuquerque, New Mexico for the annual meeting of the National Coalition of Motorcyclists and was presented the Silver Spoke Award for his work as a journalist covering actions against American motorcycle clubs. In 2012, he was flown to Baltimore, Maryland, where he was the keynote speaker at the largest Tamil Sangam in the United States. He was invited to the prestigious event to talk about his reports on the 2009 civil war in Sri Lanka, which brought a level of understanding to Americans about the heinous, genocidal acts of aggression carried out

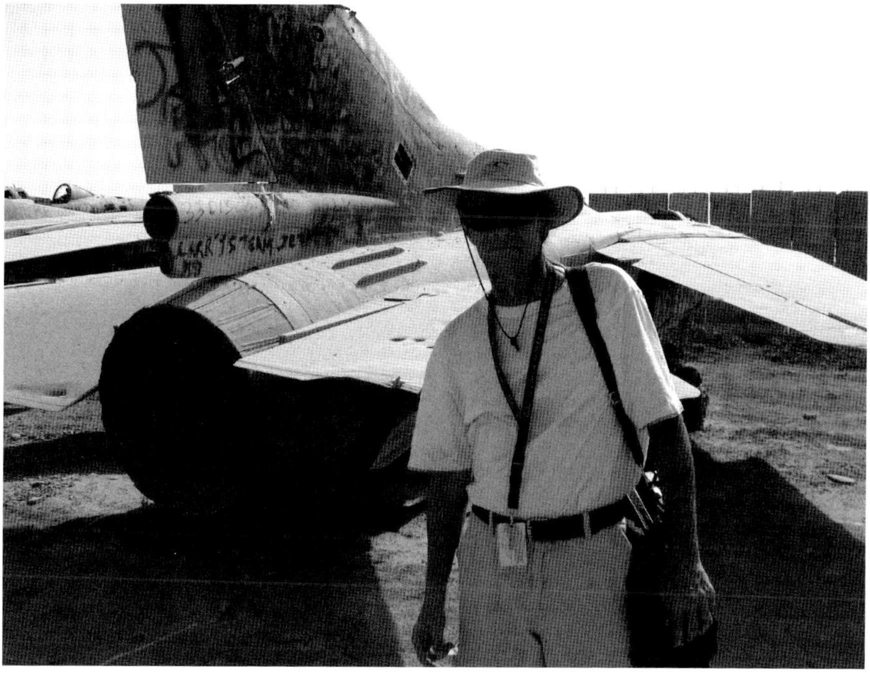

Tim King as a reporter covering the Iraq War in 2008. *Courtesy of Colonel Todd Farmer, Oregon National Guard.*

by the Sri Lankan Sinhala Buddhist government and military against an embattled religious minority.

In 2013, Tim King and Robert O'Dowd published the book *Betrayal* about crimes committed by officials within the U.S. Marine Corps. Tim and Bob both served as Marines at the now-closed Marine Corps Air Station El Toro, which several years ago was named an EPA Superfund site for vast toxic contamination. At least thirty-five known cancer-causing carcinogens are found in the groundwater beneath the old base. Countless cancer cases and deaths are tied to this stalwart of government irresponsibility.

In 2013, Tim took an 11,500-mile national solo motorcycle ride across the country, giving talks about military base contamination, post-traumatic stress disorder and Agent Orange and the problems Vietnam veterans and their descendants are afflicted with.

The following year, Tim rode his motorcycle through several states in an effort to promote *Betrayal*, connecting with Robert O'Dowd and the Veterans for Peace group in Salt Lake City, Utah. He and Bob gave talks about the book and veteran's health issues.

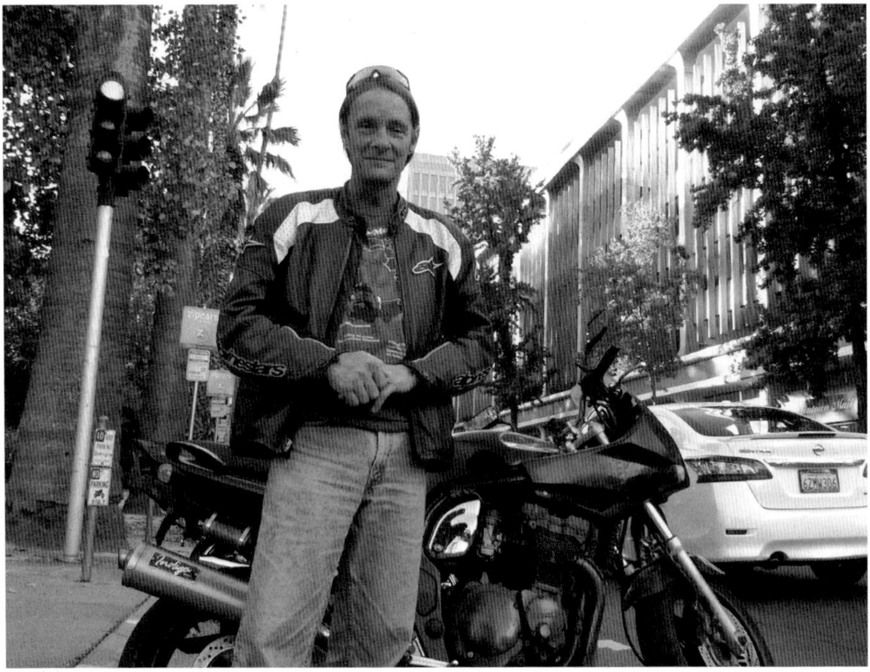

Photo by Tom King.

In 2015, Tim launched Salem Ghost Tours in Oregon, where he continues to write news articles and, he says, "take super interesting people out on mind-numbing haunted history tours."

In December 2016, Tim King answered the call again. Wesley Clark Jr. organized the Standing Rock Veterans event in Standing Rock, South Dakota, where native people had been fighting for several months to block the Dakota Access Pipeline (DAPL). Tim was one of thousands of U.S. vets who made the trip and stood side by side with the Lakota Sioux in defending the precious waterway. It is history now, but the showing of veterans led to the U.S. Secretary of the Army blocking the project. Of course, the presidential administration changed, and DAPL is moving forward again. But Tim said it was one of his proudest moments, seeing fellow vets from all over not just the United States but also the world come to the aid of America's indigenous people.

Tim is the father of five sons: Matthew, Nathan, Austin, Sean and Christian.